POETRY

In the Blood

Cortège

From the Devotions

Pastoral

The Tether

Rock Harbor

The Rest of Love

Riding Westward

Quiver of Arrows: Selected Poems, 1986–2006

Speak Low

Double Shadow

Silverchest

Reconnaissance

Wild Is the Wind

Star Map with Action Figures (chapbook)

Pale Colors in a Tall Field

Firsts: 100 Years of Yale Younger Poets (editor)

PROSE

Coin of the Realm: Essays on the Life and Art of Poetry

The Art of Daring: Risk, Restlessness, Imagination

TRANSLATION

Sophocles: *Philoctetes*

Then the War

FARRAR STRAUS GIROUX

NEW YORK

CARL PHILLIPS

THEN THE WAR

AND SELECTED POEMS,

2007-2020

Farrar, Straus and Giroux
120 Broadway, New York 10271

The Library of Congress has cataloged the hardcover edition as follows:
Names: Phillips, Carl, 1959- author.
Title: Then the war : and selected poems, 2007-2020 / Carl Phillips.
Description: First edition. | New York : Farrar, Straus and Giroux, 2022. |
   Includes bibliographical references and index.
Identifiers: LCCN 2021042469 | ISBN 9780374603762 (hardcover)
Subjects: LCGFT: Poetry.
Classification: LCC PS3566.H476 T47 2022 | DDC 811/.54—dc23/eng/20211018
LC record available at https://lccn.loc.gov/2021042469

Paperback ISBN: 978-0-374-60767-8

Designed by Crisis
Title-page and part-opener photograph
copyright © by Carl Phillips

www.fsgbooks.com
www.twitter.com/fsgbooks
www.facebook.com/fsgbooks

3 5 7 9 10 8 6 4

Contents

2

SELECTED POEMS, 2007-2020

Star Map with Action Figures

THEN

THE

WAR

THEN THE
WAR

1

Invasive Species

Switchgrass beachgrass trespass
little song. Little song years remastering truth
    now begins its own truth little song

deep in the night. Not a wreath more a
    crown little song worn shyly. Past
regret little song no weep remembering

    nor long for. Little song done with tears
though nowhere anyone not somehow hand
    in hand little song still lonely undaunted un-
persuaded. Persuasion a meadow once

    violence the field
seeding itself with its own flower. For fist
    little song. Up from the dragged lake of the singer's throat
little song severed fist in the light turning. It shines in the light.

Of California

We'd gone out walking among the sycamores. The dragonfruit
cactuses, ornamenting the yards we walked past, hadn't
flowered yet, but soon would, the way what isn't love—at all—
can begin to feel like love. It can seem impossible that it will find,
like the dragonfruit, if not forgotten entirely, its place-in-memory
with so many other things that used to hold importance. They
scarcely matter now. Why remember,
                                        at all? There's a wind I call
more deliberate, what the deer in flight makes, for example,
a physics of muscle times the speed with which, dividing air,
the deer rushes through it; and there's another wind, that just
happens. It moved easily among the sycamores. It made a sound
like a mouth repeating over and over, as if somehow stuck, what I
mistook, as he did,
                      for the word *senseless*, but no—*sexless*: that was it.
I couldn't decide whether what was meant was a kind of freedom
or something more along the lines of how, apparently, most people
live: plenty of agony, sure, in their faces, but not a trace of
the sweeter kind, the kind worth suffering for, just a little, that can
make suffering itself seem no different from any other country
at war that, waking to, we've only to look down upon from a tower,
say, or a high rampart, to understand how much smaller it is than,
in dream,
          we'd thought. They say the absence of a thing doesn't
have to mean the desire for it. That's the trouble with words: soon
almost anything sounds true. This is my body, he said, lying down

on the grass, if by lying down can be meant also what looked like
offering me one last bright chance to believe in forgiveness as a
sturdy enough box for containing rescue. Yes, and these
are my hands, I said back, holding them out but

slightly away from him,

lest he confuse presentation with any need, on my part, for his
appraisal. I lay beside him. Each of us silent, though for different
reasons. Neither touched the other. The strict, the elegant sycamore-
shadows of California swept our faces, but did not touch them.

That the Gods Must Rest

That the gods must rest doesn't mean that they stop existing.
Is that true? Do you believe it's true?

                              I could tell it was morning
by all the crows rising again from that otherwise abandoned husk
of a car over there—so ruined, who can tell the make of it now,
what color. Or maybe if being stranded on a wind farm at night
with no stars to sing to could be a color—that color, maybe . . .
The way an unexpectedly fine idea will sometimes emerge from
what looked on the outside like the mind as usual treading water
was the crows, rising. A misleading clarity to the air, like logic:
he only wants what he deserves; he deserves everything he wants;
I deserve all I've ever built and fought for; we deserve our loneliness.

The Enchanted Bluff

You can see here, though the marks
are faint, how the river must once have coincided
with love's most eastern boundary. But it's years now
since the river shifted, as if done with the same
view both over and over
                    and never twice, which
is to say, done at last with conundrum, when it's
just a river—here's a river . . . Why not say so,
why this need to name things based on what
they remind us of—cattail and broom, skunk
cabbage—or on what
                  we wished for: heal-all;
forget-me-not. Despite her dyed-too-black hair
wildly haloing her shoulders, not a witch, caftanned
in turquoise, gold, turning men into better men,
into men with feelings—instead, just my mother,
already gone crazy a bit, watching the yard fill
with the feral cats
              that she fed each night.
Who says you can't die from regret being all
you can think about? What's it matter, now, if she
learned the hard way the difference finally between
freedom and merely
             setting a life free? As much
as I can, anyway, I try to keep regret far from me,
though like any song built to last, there's a

rhythm to it that, once recognized, can be hard
to shake: one if by fear, with its double flower—
panic, ambition; two if by what's the worst thing
you've ever done?

Little Shields, in Starlight

Maybe there's no need for us to go anywhere more far
than here, said the dogwood leaves, mistaking speech
for song, to the catalpa leaves, imitating silence. It was like
sex when, push the tenderness to either side of it, it's
just sex; hardly sex at all . . . Hardly worth mentioning,
except forgetting seems so much a shame, lately, and why

shouldn't there be records, however small, of our having
felt something without for once having to name it, I know
what my dirt is, as if that were enough, might well
even have to be, to have moved mostly with the best
intentions, at least, before we stopped, that's
all that happens, I think; we stop moving forever.

Morning in the Bowl of Night

■

ALMA THOMAS, 1973

Careful. The snow looks solid here, where it isn't, quite.
Beneath the snow, the earth—in that earth language
that used to be what we meant when we said silence—
says "I never left" and "I'll be back." Words that,
as if they were questions, the stripped sycamores keep
trying to answer, and failing to. That dialect that marks
the deciduous in a time without leaves—how useless it is,
mostly, the way beauty can sometimes seem to be,
all that falling upon the field of intimacy, then
getting up, just to fall back down again, you crying
right there in front of him as you hadn't before, ever,
and have not done since . . .

■

There will always be those for whom apology's
just defiance felt backward—but too late, and a bit
halfheartedly. Best to put, between them and yourself,
a distance, you'll be able to tell it's the correct distance
when their faces no longer look like faces, more a trail of
hoofprints that abruptly end, as if whatever animal,
having made it this far, had been Ganymeded upward
into sky, and past that. The trick is to make it seem—

all the time while quietly moving farther away—that
nothing's changed: the winter trees, as usual; the usual
wind, now and then, through them. Lanterns in the trees,
there should everywhere be lanterns. Let the branches imitate
a crown. It should look like memorizing what a crown once was.

■

The light stands
like a panel of glass. Frameless. Detachment on one side,
on the other side, fear. This could be the farthest
you've ever known from cruelty. It's as if you've been
singled out, somehow, exceptional, that's what
you tell yourself, though there's a present calm that
cannot calm the past. Nothing calms it. Careful. Look at
the shadows of clouds moving across the ice that still
sheets the pond, how they seem to move, as well, just
beneath the ice, like something trapped there,
private and flourishing.

Blue-Winged Warbler

They say that deep in the interstices

where dream and waking dream and what, between the two, I've
called a life, seem a nest of swords,
each crossing the other, flashless, as from long neglect,

there's a meadow's worth left, still, of the aftergrass
that grows in sweeter once the first hay-crop's been cut down, just
believe in it hard enough,

everything's findable, even now, they say (parallel, ascending), but
that's not true; not true.

Not Wild, Merely Free

It's long ago, now, since I changed forever, with just a handful of words,
a man's life. Ruined it, I'm pretty sure
he'd call it, as if to do so could be to make it fact.

But the bee's survival, as I understand it, depends in part on its ability
to distinguish colors; that, too, is a fact.
So?

    Also, that the paths people make, over time, in parks,
by departing from the paths actually designated to be walked on
are known as desire lines,
as in: I'd rather walk *here*, or lie *there*,
in that open clearing the path leads away from,

as if the point about desire was the choosing, mainly,
when it's not. It isn't.

          The back-and-forth shadows that the leaves now,
while the light's behind them, mark the bedroom's wall with,
may as well be who I was, then—not so different from what I seem
this morning: the shadows of leaves,

              not the leaves
themselves that, once the light's moved on, will still be there, at rest
or not so much, in the dark that renders shadow
all but meaningless, like song

inside the throats of mourning doves when asleep,

what they used to call rain doves, whose coloring, at the throat

especially, means one thing, I'm told, though it stands for another.

He Didn't Raise Hand or Voice

Maybe so. Or maybe it's only memory, in the end, that turns
some men into flags—anything from ownership to conquest
to Here I stopped to rest, once, but I couldn't stay—while
others, years later, past the otherwise

                           mistake of them,
become reliable compasses we still half hold on to, their
bodies a forest when seen from the air in a small plane,
so that it's possible to get close enough to see where the oaks
give way to poplar trees, or where, if you follow the pines
far enough, they open out to a field across which you can see
the ocean, we couldn't have found our way here

                                without them:
in which case, where lies mistake, at this point, and where
revision? Last night, a friend asked if I could say, even roughly,
how many men I've ever slept with; and when, unable to,
I panicked, he assured me my situation is not uncommon.
Tonight I'm not

                  so sure. The lord gives to each of us only what
we can bear, says my father, during the weekly phone call
where I practice limiting myself to a single drink—one way,
I guess, of maybe keeping my hand in when it comes
to restraint. For once, I don't push back at him, his faith;
if I can give him

that much, why shouldn't I? If I say the giving
feels, impossibly, just before I let go of it, almost like love, that's
all I'm saying. It happened; and now it's over. They moved
together in groups, and singly. They moved among the trees
as among the parts of a language they'd forgotten they knew.

In a Field, at Sunset

When he asked if I still loved him, I didn't answer;

    but of course, I loved him.

He'd become, by then, like the rhyme between lost

    and most.

The Difficulty

It's as if the difficulty were less what happened—
the truth, presumably—than how little
what happened resembles the *story*
　　of what happened. And yet the sea
　　　　has never been an ocean, even if across both—
　　　　　　given the wind, and imagination—each
　　　　　　wave can seem an end approaching,
　　　　like something holy, to be turned away from
　　(as the compass falters, stops squarely
between what's beautiful
and what was awful) or to be faced but—
　　either way—delicately, bravely; with adoration, almost.

In a Low Voice, Slowly

So stubborn, and as if almost necessary, this
    little wind, playing the leaves, their surfaces, playing
the leaves where they lie fallen, while not once
    rearranging them. Like being asked what, if anything,
do you regret at this point; and, as answer, shaping
    your own smallish song around how knowing isn't
understanding, isn't mystery either, which isn't *un*-knowing,
    not exactly, more like deciding to turn abruptly
east after so many years westering, what kind of answer
    was that? Sometimes the past seems the stuff of heraldry,
figures proper on a ground of good and evil. Other times
    the past sways ocean-like above me. There's a sound
deer still make when in sixes they come down
    from the hills at sunrise, the kind of sunrise where
no sun's visible, but it's daylight, and just the rain, and
    the deer passing like their own form of light through it;
their hooves mark the damp ground incidentally,
    no particular meaning. It's true that love marks the body.

Fixed Shadow, Moving Water

One friend tells me everything's political,
another says nothing is, we just make it political.
By "we," he means human beings, I assume—
     what's political to a fox curled in sleep,
or a pond, or a sycamore in winter with no leaves left
to stop the snow falling through it? I have loved you
     for less time than I have loved some others,
but none more deeply than you; no one more
absolutely. Which, as if inevitably, amounts
     to a hierarchy of sorts, doesn't it? Value,
then the power that comes with it—soon enough,
the distribution of power, who gets to do the distributing . . .

     But if we make of tenderness a countervailing force, the two of us—

     If we can make, *from* tenderness, a revolution—

Somewhere, right now, a hawk

has just entered a meadow's
airspace, and in turn the meadow
becomes all but noiseless. You're

asleep, finally. The competing
fears that cross your face routinely
at last give way, not to innocence

exactly, maybe more a freedom
from having to be anyone
to anyone—that alone, but

this time not minding it. Is it true
that only by having first passed
through absolute despair

can we arrive at anything close
to self-knowing? Are birds in dreams
still considered dangerous

because they mean possibility?
Now when I say body, it's as if
to correct myself for what I missed

before, looking elsewhere.
I'm a song, changing. I'm a light
rain falling through a vast

darkness toward a different
darkness. It could be anything—
the earth; it could be the sea.

Sing a Darkness

Slowly the fog did what fog does, eventually: it lifted, the way
veils tend to at some point in epic
    verse so that the hero can
see the divinity at work constantly behind
all things mortal, or that's
    the idea, anyway, I'm not saying I do or don't
believe that, I'm not even sure that belief can change
any of it, at least in terms of the facts of how,
    moment by moment, any life unfurls, we can
call it fate or call it just what happened, what
happens, while we're busy trying to *describe*
    or *explain* what happens,
how a mimosa tree caught growing close beside a house
gets described as "hugging the house,"
    for example, as if an impulse to find affection everywhere
made us have to put it there,
a spell against indifference,
    as if that were the worst thing—
is it?
Isn't it?
    The fog lifted.
It was early spring, still.
The dogwood brandished those pollen-laden buds
    that precede a flowering. History. What survives, or doesn't.
How the healthiest huddled, as much at least
as was possible, more closely together,

to give the sick more room. How they mostly all died, all the same.

I was nowhere I'd ever been before.

Nothing mattered.

I practiced standing as still as I could, for as long as I could.

AMONG THE TREES

What happened back there, among the trees, is only as untenable as you allow yourself or just decide to believe it is. It happened, and now it's over. And the end feels—to you, at least—both like the end of a long pilgrimage and like the end of a well-reasoned, irrefutable argument, which is its own form of pilgrimage: don't both depend on stamina and faith, in the right proportions? Wasn't the point, at the end, persuasion?

■

I used to speak in terms of shadowlands, by which I meant, I think, some space where what transpires between two bodies and what gets transacted almost look the same. I'd say a thing like

> There's a kind of shadowland that one body makes, entering
> another; and there's a shadowland the body contains always
> within itself, without resolution—as mystery a little more
> often, perhaps, should be . . .

and I'd call it a poem, and it looked like one, but how it felt was more like saying aloud the words *rescue me* long enough that it almost seemed plausible that mere saying could turn the light to twilight, and the twilight dark. I lived in the world that, for lack of a prettier word, I'd call tangible, where risk meant risk, it seemed, and violation violation, not psychological but solid things, for they each cast a shadow as only a solid thing, so I'd been told, could, though I had tried to touch them—violation, risk—and each time my hands touched nothing.

■

My earliest memory of trees is of a particular fig tree in the yard of the first house I remember, in Portland, Oregon. I was five, at the most. Sometimes what I remember is playing in the shade of it, and at other times the bees that seemed to bloom from inside the windfalls—though it seems now to have been less the wind that brought the fruit down but the weight of ripeness itself, as if sweetness, too much sweetness, meant mistake, punishment therefore; for hours, I'd watch the bees enter and leave the split-open sides, and how the figs looked lonely, once the bees had gone, as if to be plundered meant at least not being alone . . .

One evening, instead of coming inside when called, I climbed the fig tree, wearing only a tee shirt and underpants. It seemed like a game, to be up in the tree, and my parents not able to find me, calling my name as they wandered the yard. And then somehow, I fell, and then suddenly stopped falling: my underwear had caught on a branch, saving me from hitting the ground, but holding me in midair, unable to get down. The way I remember it, my mother told my father to get a ladder.

What's very clear in memory is my father saying I should hang there in the tree for a bit, to learn a lesson about disobeying my parents.

I find no evidence, in my sixty years of knowing him, that my father is particularly attentive to historical resonances when it comes to our daily lives, but I can't help thinking about the place of trees in African-American history, as the site for lynching. How strange for my father, an African American, to find it a fitting punishment to leave his son hanging in a tree at night.

My earliest memory of humiliation is of a particular fig tree in the yard of the first house I remember. Who can say how related this is to my refusal, all my life, to believe forgiveness exists?

■

Some trees are compasses, and some are flags. If a flag tells you where you are, a compass can potentially tell you how to get there or how to find someplace else. A flag, in marking a spot, seems more definitive, a form of punctuation; a compass implies movement, navigation. I know a man who, whenever he needs to write, or cry, or think—*really* think— goes to a willow in his local park and hides beneath its draped branches. He goes there so often, you could almost say he's become *part* of the willow; he seems a willow himself; he marks a place in my life where I stopped to rest, once, but I couldn't stay. Then there's another man, long ago now. His body a forest when seen from the air in a small plane, so that it's possible to get close enough to see where the oaks give way to poplar trees, or where, if you follow the pines far enough, they'll open out to a field across which you can see the ocean. I couldn't have found my way here without him.

■

Despite my childhood mishap with the fig tree, and despite fairy tales, in which the forest so often contains danger—witches ready to shove children into ovens, wolves masquerading as harmless grandmothers—I've had a love of trees all my life. Throughout high school, I lived in a house in the woods in Massachusetts, and even on the darker mornings of winter what kept me from being frightened were the trees themselves— mostly scrub pines, as we called them there, with struggling oaks scattered among them. Unlike the kids at school, the trees remained silent as I passed, and I took this as a sign of acceptance. Irrational, sure—but in my feeling so unlike everyone else at school, in my confused wrestling with what I felt was real but I couldn't name precisely, why not take silence for acceptance? Among the trees loneliness could be itself, in the open—so could strangeness—even as both remained hidden from the rest of the world for the time it took me to pass through the woods to the bus stop. As I walked, I'd sing to the trees, loudly at first, then more and more softly the closer I got to where the woods gave out, until all I could hear was whatever wind there was through the leaves and needles. A sound like the trees unable to sing back, but trying to.

■

As with myth, fairy tales often seem designed to explain something very real in surreal terms. The story of Red Riding Hood might as easily be a way to warn about the fact of dangerous animals in the woods as to suggest that potential criminals might be encountered. The secrecy that a forest provides makes it the perfect setting for crime. Also for intimacy, which has often been deemed a crime. It makes sense that woods and forests have long been a queer space. Queer, not just in the sense of strangeness or alienation—going back to my relationship to the woods in high school—but in terms of sexuality, the woods as a space in which to hunt for sex. What is cruising, if not a form of hunting, if not to pass, as animal (the act of sex is perhaps our most animal manifestation, as humans), in pursuit of another human who has chosen for the moment to yield more entirely to the animal that each of us carries inside?

■

Was like when the body surrenders to risk, that moment when an unwillingness to refuse can seem no different from an inability to, though they are not the same—inability, unwillingness. To have said otherwise doesn't make it true, or even make it count as true. Yes, but what does the truth matter now, I whispered, stepping further inside what, by then, was night, almost. The tamer animals would soon lie down again, and the wild go free.

■

It's not just the convenience of the woods—its ability to conceal, to keep a secret—that makes it a likely site for sexual behavior that isn't societally condoned. Trees are utterly natural, or the collections of trees called woods and forests tend, anyway, not to have been artificially constructed (as compared with parks or public gardens). And this natural context for sexual intimacy can give, if not a sense of wholesomeness exactly, then a sense of permission, at least, to what can feel like—what we've been made to feel *is*—transgression; if only temporarily, the trees erase the shame that drove us to seek hiddenness in the first place. Or if shame didn't drive us there, a reasonable fear likely did. And then—remember?—that well-worn path where we found one another, the trees to either side like a lengthy convoy of fears that kept diminishing, the more south they shuffled—until there *was* no fear.

■

At this point in my life, I'm not always sure how much of what I think about my life among trees—in forests, in woods—actually happened, how much is imagined, and how much is what I've read and somehow super-imposed over my own actual experience—everything from *Sir Gawain and the Green Knight*—the forest as the site of quest and conquest, riddle and answer—to those passages in Tolkien's *The Hobbit* and *The Lord of the Rings* where so much travel is done under cover of night through for-ests. In the Tolkien, especially, while there is plenty of potential danger, so many of the scenes have to do with camaraderie and trust and an in-timacy that isn't sexual at all. Or I think about Randall Jarrell, whose po-etry often revisits fairy tale, and seems especially fascinated with what goes on in the woods—specifically, Jarrell seems to want to rewrite fairy tale and the psychology of it. The forest is an example of "the lost world" that he's always seeking, where the witch who would kill children is transformed. Here's the end of his "The House in the Wood":

> Here at the bottom of the world, what was before the world
> And will be after, holds me to its black
>
> Breasts and rocks me: the oven is cold, the cage is empty,
> In the House in the Wood, the witch and her child sleep.

The house is held by the wood, the mother and child are held by the house, perhaps the mother is holding her child. Which is to say the poem's in part about enclosure as a form of security, and about nurture, the very opposite of what the witch conventionally stands for. The wood, in effect, reverses evil to the good it began as, or that's the wish, a human one, with which the wood in the end has very little to do. In that same poem Jarrell reminds us that

> after the last leaf,
> The last light—for each year is leafless,
>
> Each day is lightless, at the last—the wood begins
> Its serious existence: it has no path,
>
> No house, no story; it resists comparison . . .

So there are the trees of literature, floating somewhere in my head, always. Then there are all of my actual adventures and misadventures among trees throughout my life. And then there are the stories that maybe began with a shred of fact but got transformed in the course of my making a poem. Jarrell, again: "Which one's the mockingbird? which one's the world?"

■

They moved together in groups, and singly.
They moved among the trees as among the parts of a language they'd forgotten they knew
Pitch pine, sycamore, maple, oak, and birch.
Humiliation, loneliness, permission, sex, and shame.
Memory, innocence, forgiveness. Willow. Willow.

■

Another way of thinking, though, about this interplay between reality and imagination when it comes to memory is that I've lost track of what happened, versus what serves as *camouflage* for what happened—camouflage in the form not just of trees but of the context they become for the stories that I tell in poems. In a sense, the poems themselves are trees, or treelike, in that they become a place where what's difficult and/or forbidden can have a place both to be hidden and within which to feel free to unfurl and extend itself. Here's how I spoke of the forest once:

> I lived, in those days, at the forest's edge—
> metaphorically, so it can sometimes seem now, though
> the forest was real, as my life beside it was. I spent
> much of my time listening to the sounds of random, un-
> knowable things dropping or being dropped from, variously,
> a middling height or a great one until, by winter, it was
> just the snow falling, each time like a new, unnecessary
> taxonomy or syntax for how to parse what's plain, snow
> from which the occasional lost hunter would emerge
> every few or so seasons, and—just once—a runaway child
> whom I gave some money to and told no one about,
>
> having promised . . .

And here is a different way since then:

> There's a forest that stands at the exact center of sorrow.
> Regrets find no shelter there.
> The trees, when they sway,

sway like the manes of horses when a storm's not far.
There's no reason to stay there,
nothing worth going to see,
but if you want to you can pass through the forest
in the better part of a long day.
Who would want to, though?

Story, versus information. Lyric, versus didactic. Long, periodic sentences, versus clipped, straightforward ones. Catalpa trees aren't hawthorns. I'm not the man I was.

■

They lay where they'd fallen, beneath the forest's canopy. And at first when they woke, it was as if the forest, besides containing them, was itself contained, as in a snow globe when it's been shaken and just now set down, except instead of snow, just shadows falling, *like* snow, in pieces that it was as useless to try to hold on to as catching snow on the tongue—To catch us is at once to know us and to lose us, said the shadows, falling like snow, gathering in shadowy, steep banks on which the light, being light, depended.

■

To know where we came from—and what we came through—doesn't have to mean we know any more clearly where we are, except not *there*, anymore. The forest begins where civilization ends, so I'd been told. Past here be monsters. Past the meadow; past harvest. Past daylight into forest light—for it's never all darkness, beneath the trees, not even at night; not even on a moonless night. Song travels differently in forest light. Everything's different.

That the forest itself contains no apology doesn't mean you're not hurt. Or I'm not sorry. Or I didn't hurt you.

Toward the end of Marilyn Nelson's poem "My Grandfather Walks in the Woods," the grandfather asks the trees a question and "They answer / with voices like wind / blowing away from him." That's one way of putting it, for their voices *can* sound like wind. What matters more, I think, is that in the language of trees there's no grammatical mood: questions, statements, commands—it's all song, stripped of anything like judgment, intention, or need. This makes translation especially difficult. Though I know parts of many of their songs, I've only three by heart: "Yes, you can tell me anything," and "No, even we can't help you," and "If I were you, I'd be the lostest, lostest boy I know."

■

In the dream, I'd bought a large house in a large city, a house that came with a backyard so thick with trees that by summer, by then in full leaf, they blocked all views of the high-rises to the north, of the neighbors to the west, while to the east through the leaves of an old pear tree I could see the cathedral dome, on top of it a cross caught the sunlight and tossed it back. Besides the pear, there's a high-rise-sized pin oak, two dogwoods, two catalpas, a chestnut, before the yard ends in a stand of bamboo I'll eventually lose almost all of, as the dream continues. When I wake, it's as if to another dream, though it feels no different: I become briefly silver, as in what the leaves mean, beneath. Bells are ringing. No, the leaves are falling. *Now* the bells start ringing. Sudden scattering, all around me, of leaves, all gold.

2

While Night Still Keeps Us

Finally, if we're very lucky, we get to see affection
for what it's always been, most likely: love's truest
season. The stars receive unto themselves again
the rogue star that sex, believing itself to be king,
for a time really was, and gift it with the steadier,
more reliable crown of context. Words like *rescue*

and *tenderness* and *forever* and *don't go*, flightless
now, swim in circles the lake of drama they only
used to appreciate for what they could see in it
of their own reflections. Too late, of course,
they know better now. They can see the shore,
but cannot reach it. They can see the cattails
that grow thick there, blown to seed, as happens,

yes, necessarily, and just beyond the cattails, rioting
as usual in banks of color, the flowering shrub
called oleander, each part of it poisonous, but most
especially the smoke that, like an unexpected
second bloom, the plant indifferently
releases, when set on fire.

Then the War

They planted flowers because the house had many rooms
and because they'd imagined a life in which
cut flowers punctuate each room, as if each were a sentence

not just to be decorated but to be given some discipline,
what the most memorable sentences—like people—always
slightly resist . . . Spit of land; rags

of cloud rack. Meanwhile,
hawk's-nest, winter-nest, stamina as a form of faith, little
cove that a life equals, what they meant, I think, by

what they called the soul, twilight taking hold
deep in the marshweed, in the pachysandra, where the wind
can't reach.

Then the war.
Then the field, and the mounted police
parading their proud-looking horses across it.

Then the next morning's fog, the groundsmen barely visible
inside it, shadowlike, shade-like,
grooming the field back to immaculateness.

Then the curtains billowing out from the lightless room
toward the sea.
Then the one without hair

stroked the one who had some. They closed their eyes.

If gently, hard to say *how* gently.

Then the war was nothing that still bewildered them, if it ever had.

As the Rain Comes Down Harder

I

That what you want
won't be at all what the gods deliver.
Worse, that there are no gods,
there's only intention—
what else explains
the power with which the escaped
falcon pulls skyward (but as if
through water, behind it) its bells
and jesses, its hood
for calming the fears that vision
always, it seems, brings
with it?

     Or does fear, instructional
     at last, clear a way
     for vision?

II

He believes in heaven, what he calls
The Halo Bar—now and then, Club Halo.
He says seafoam's more a mood, really, than a color.
He believes there's a landscape inside the body that contains

the self, what gives to the body its own distinctiveness. Says
this accounts for how some people, seeing an abyss, see one more
thing to practice falling into, while others instead set up camp
beside it. Hard not to love that way of thinking,
or him, to be honest. When I actually told him so, once—
the part about him, I mean—he stayed quiet, at first; then he said
Each face wears fear differently. As if that were an answer. And maybe it was.
He says where he comes from the sign for peace can also mean
a swan, sleeping: he makes a fist with his left hand; with his right, he covers it.

Something to Believe In

My two hunting dogs have names, but I rarely use them. As
I go, *they* go: I lead; they follow, the blue-eyed one first, then
the one whose coloring—her coat, not her eyes—I sometimes
call never-again-o-never-this-way-henceforth. Hope, ambition:
these are not their names, though the way they run might suggest
otherwise. Like steam off night-soaked wooden fencing when
the sun first hits it, they rise each morning at my command. Late
in the *Iliad*, Priam the king of Troy predicts his own murder—
correctly, except it won't be by spear, as he imagines, but by
sword thrust. He can see his corpse, sees the dogs he's fed and
trained so patiently pulling the corpse apart. After that, he says,
When they're full, they'll lie in the doorway, they'll lap my blood.
I say: Why shouldn't they? Everywhere, the same people who
mistake obedience for loyalty think somehow loyalty weighs more
than hunger, when it doesn't. At night, when it's time for bed,
we sleep together, the three of us: muscled animal, muscled animal,
muscled animal. The dogs settle to either side of me as if each
were the slightly folded wing of a beast from fable, part power, part
recognition. We breathe in a loose kind of unison. Our breathing
ripples the way oblivion does—routinely, across history's face.

The Blue Door

Not every field was a forest once. That's a myth, a kind of story—
call it snowfall, spring, October, all that's left, sometimes, of
history, to explain history. Likewise, approximate doesn't always

have to mean less true: think of how often as close as we could get,
or ever hoped to, wound up *being* the truth. You're all I've got,
he said to me once, or maybe I said it—to no one, maybe. Sure,

it's hard not knowing what exactly to be afraid of; but that we
recognize pattern—that it comforts us—that's what makes pattern
dangerous. Plastic flags in a steady wind, sustained applause, wasps

settling into the juniper, rising from it . . . As if meaning refused, by
definition, chaos. In general, the hunter's eye moves first toward
what's *not* perfect. The blue door, half shut, at the end of a lie

that includes horses. How easily, tonight, the sea's motion makes it
almost forgettable that the stars reflected there have their own motion.

Rough Surf in Moonlight

As for power, it won't be won, I think,
by restraint this time. Power that shifts like a ripped
    page blown about in traffic. Page torn from some
rare and patiently illuminated manuscript: excerpts
    from paradise; angels depicted as hammers of bronze
thrown skyward—though no hand visible—
    and staying there. For a moment, pursuit seems
no better or worse a strategy than retreat. I believe
    the real sorrow, when it comes, will not be this one.

Like the Sweet Wet Earth Itself

And after sex: as after rain, a clarity that, though by now proverbial,

could still surprise. Indeed, it did surprise him. All over again,
he could feel, through and through, what most live their entire
lives merely understanding: about apology not erasing cruelty;
about forgiveness not erasing what lingers, shimmering, in cruelty's
measureless wake; about erasure not being the point, finally, one more
version of wishing backward—which is to say,

　　　　　　　　　　　　　　too late . . . The adult
cicada is not the shell-of-itself that it leaves behind. The spent casing
has nothing to do, now, with the bullet lodged in the deer's throat,
the deer long since split open, dressed, hung by hooks, to drain,
from the barn's blue rafters. Evidence is not the same
as memory. He'd forgotten, years ago, the question; but the answer—

it never left him, or hardly ever: *Yes; for the lion's foot, too, is feathered.*

On Coming Close

The horses we rode: they must all be dead by now.
But the self—who I was *then*—can almost seem
unchanged, still, if I meet no mirrors to allow
what's outside to betray what's in; if I think of
regret as I've always thought of it, no more useful
than apology, no less impossible to believe in
than forgiveness; if I forget—as I tend to—regret's
powers . . .

         Without mirrors, my eyes are the color
of river water crossing a bed of stones, river stones,
in summer. Without mirrors, I can almost say yes:
yes to holiness, the river lower than usual, because
summer, but the sky Novembering, so the water
the color of what's from the start been at once
unknowable,

               yet understood, somehow. Not
one of those horses ever came even close
to that color—being horses; not rivers. Which
makes me want to forgive them, just a little, in
spite of myself. Or to say I loved some small part
of even the worst of them. Love— Isn't love
what they used to call holiness once, long ago, on earth?

Electric

It's a calm night. The kind of calm inside which,
hours after having entered another's body with your own
body, you wonder Did that happen, any of it, and then the staggering away
home from it, as from a crime scene, or the grottoed site of some
miracle believed in by enough pilgrims to make it seem
almost true? . . . It's as if the calm

contains the night, which contains
the fears that only exist, finally, inside
you. Each fear being different, each contains
its own dream—is *dream* the word? *Vision*, maybe? Except invisible,
the way certain gestures are, the gesture of sorrow when it shifts, the way
a storm shifts, to something easier to bear

than sorrow. A hawk tearing not so slowly at a smaller bird that's
still breathing. A man thinking that by withdrawing from the conversation,
he's taken control of the conversation. I've known more than a few men
like that. Sex in colors. Names like Believe me or don't, whatever. Tattoos like
Dangerous. And Don't disturb. And It's a long life,
if you're lucky. And You were right

all along: It *was* love. And I wish you more time. And When they most
needed bandaging, he covered my eyes. The skin of his hands. Like deerskin.

Soft Western Light

There are places where it's still
possible to watch bees map
a garden out with what
used to be called industry
in a language that feels

each day less and less
my own. But the dream
of exile turns out
mostly to have been
a false one: me cutting

the weaker parts routinely
away from what, set a bit
more free that way, might
more likely flourish;
it seems it's better,

to flourish . . . To confine
desire to what holds
sweetness—how small desire
would be. In the more
reliable dream (but

who's to say more true)
I'm just a body like any

other in the world,
in motion. The leaves shift
slightly as I pass beneath them—

not acknowledgment, but
like that. It's as if they cared
for me, or felt at least
they should seem to care. I'll miss
you too.

Everything All of It

The understory here seems a mix
    entirely of Virginia creeper, wild
        parsley, and what looks to be mint

by its flower, but it's not mint, I know
    it's not. That's just appearances. Like
        those mounted antlers that, in the right

light, cast a shadow that can look a
    lot like one animal chasing another,
        though in play or for survival, it's

hard to tell. Or the way detachment
    can resemble confidence, a form of
        bravery almost, until the weather shifts,

and there's just the usual wrecked
    cathedral of the mind, pierced over
        and over again with fear and sorrow,

what feels like sorrow. Less by design
    than circumstance, my corruptions
        have been mostly private. I've always

loved how—unlike *some* trees that,
    having grown too tall and therefore
        too heavy, fall over, uprooting themselves

—oak trees at a certain age begin
    routinely losing, on purpose, some of
        their branches: the roots, so much older

now, can only bear so much weight. I
    get that. What our lives amount to
        doesn't have to be the same as what

we make of our lives. I like to think
    that's true. If I tell you most of it's
        pretty much been dream, it's because I have to.

Blurry Finally in Too Soon Each of Us

A water-meadow is not a flood-meadow.

A working meadow's not a fallow field.

Heartbreak like a bloodhound better off abandoned because untamable.

There's a slant of light I used to call Self-Portrait as a Lion, Bringing Down a Stag.

Only Portions of the Map Still Legibly Survive

Having had their moment or, if luckier, the better part
of a day in the sun as proverbed, it was time to move on.
Some died, not because of this,

                      but as if so. Some retreated
into the memory of their earlier triumphs, others chose
not so much to remember as to fill those in who had never
known of said triumphs, having been born so much past
all of that—what can history be

                      expected to mean, honestly,
to those who scarcely have any history, yet, of their own?
But the waning of influence is not the same as a loss of power—
it doesn't have to be, said the wisest who, understanding this,
found their trust where they'd always put it, in what by
sheer definition is all but impossible to argue with, or
against: detachment. Look at us now,

                      entering our days
no differently than we did before: pity in one hand,
for the few who with time may come to deserve it; and
in the other hand, an indifference that,

                      with enough
practice, detachment leads to, though that was never
the plan, not on our part, an indifference we've wielded
so long we forget it's

                      there, almost, until something
reminds us: gulls scattering before us, say, the way
the letters that *spell* loneliness can scatter, eventually,

as if weary with meaning—with having *had* to mean—
from what loneliness really deep down feels like:
magnetic, unignorable; why,

            the waves themselves bow down.

Archery

was still a thing, then. To have timed your arrow
perfectly meant watching the air for a moment
seem stitched throughout with a kind of
timelessness. To have straddled at last, correctly,
the storm of falling in love (and staying there) meant
the smell of apples, victory, tangerines, and smoke
all mixed together on the breath

of a stranger, half asleep still, just beginning to remember a bit,
as he stirs beside you. I dreamed we were young again,
he's mumbling, as if to someone whose name he's known
long enough to have called it out more than once in anger
and sex and fear equally. Somewhere happiness too,

right? All those hours spent trying to outstare the distance
of what the days must come to,

and pretending a choice to it: now the shadow-script
that willows and hazel trees mark the barn's western
face with; now the wind-rippled field, like a lesser version—tamer,
tamable—of the sea, for movement (same infinite
pattern, and variation; randomness and intention; release;
restraint—that kind of movement) . . .

                              Dear saddle
of gentleness. Dear moss, sweet moss that only

the dark and wet and patience make possible. To sing a song
of water, and not drown in it. And some calling that
a good trick. And some calling it

mastery. That last flickering before nightfall. From beneath
the low branches. I dreamed we were new again. Stars. Just a little
past dusk.

Initial Descent

As for the mixed colors of the so-called autumn
of a life—*his* life, colors like kindness and unkindness and
"You've trusted me this far; listen carefully: don't trust me"—

he kept walking bravely into them. The leaves fell everywhere
around him, as if hoping, impossibly, to change the definition
for a bit when it comes to leaves, to the power of leaves, and

then to power itself: kinetic bruise of, exacting tenderness
with which, without which; power when (the smoke
done clearing, the air done trembling) it still radiates

—felt, but unseen, untouchable—from the forge
of Eros, who knows full well the difference between disaster,
disappointment, joy, but doesn't care about it.
No one here cares, who matters;
there's just the one bright, flashing hammer of love, like always.

To Autumn

Whatever it is that, some nights,
can rescue cricket song from
becoming just more of the usual
    white noise—tonight, it's working.
The hours toss with the apparent
weightlessness of leaves when each
    leaf seems, for once, its own dream,
not part of the larger, more general
dream of leaves being limited to tossing
    with either diminishment
or renewal, when why should those
be the only choices? What about joy,
    and despair? What about
ambition?

           If wild, I was once
more gentle. There's a version of
    autumn where the stars' reflections
on the river tonight look, at one moment,
like freight thrown overboard;
    at the next, like signal lights cast up
through water by a city submerged
where the river's deepest. There's
    another version. Holiness has
no limits, there, only two requirements:
to be hidden; to adore what's hidden.

Of the Shining Underlife

Above me, the branches toss toward and away from each other
the way privacy does with what ends up
showing, despite ourselves, of
who we are, inside.

Then they're branches again—hickory, I think.

—It's not too late, then.

Anywhere Like Peace

He's unbuttoning his shirt, we've never met before, he says
last night he had a dream about me. A good dream,
he tells me; a strong one—meaning *I* was strong, and that for the first
time in years, apparently, he felt completely safe. To confuse
closure with conclusion is nothing new, I at first
want to say to him, but a
                              shadow-softness to his face brings out
a softness in me that I don't show, usually, it makes me
want to lean hard into his chest instead, the part where the hair—
faint, still, as if still filling in—looks like two wings
positioned where they shouldn't be, but on purpose, so that
flight means for once not seeing the earth fall away, but the sky
getting steadily closer, let the body
                              approach . . . Will I ever
stop wanting more than what I've already got, I used to wonder,
not realizing yet that's all ambition *is*, finally; I thought
humility would be a smaller thing, a quieter
thing, it seems I was wrong about that, too. I can't
decide if it's just my being so much older now, or if it's
always been true, that winter foliage
is the prettiest foliage.

Entire Known World So Far

What's meant to be wind emerges from what's
presumably a god's mouth, as if people
thought that way, once, as I have read they did,
though I have never believed it. Yes,
the stag inexplicably there, on a raft
at sea, how the light catches in the runneled
fur of a dog's underpaws as he steers
across dream; yes, the gods and their
signs, if you want, everywhere—

but the wind is the wind. The map makes
the world seem like a human body
when it's been stripped and you can finally
see it for the world it is: plunderable—

almost, in places, as if asking for it—

who *wouldn't* want to lay waste to it,
the map suggests, suggest the hands
that made the map, with the kind of
grace that proves grace can
be a sturdiness, too.

∎

But the world is *not* like a human body.

Or the dark that, just past twilight, overtakes a canyon.

Or the shiver of sleigh bells on the collar
of an invisible donkey, scratching itself
in the dark,
in the cold of it—

        donkey bells . . .

Night Comes and Passes Over Me

There's a rumor of light that
any dark starts off as. Plato speaks
here and there of colors, but only
once, I think, does he break them
down into black and white, red,
and a fourth color. By then they'd
reached the California high country
where, knowing none of the names for
all the things that grew there, they

began to make names up. But to have
trained an animal to come just a bit
closer because here, here's blood,
doesn't mean you've tamed it. Trans-
lations vary for what Plato calls his
fourth color: what comes closest
to a combination of (since they
aren't the same) radiant and
bright—what shifting water does,

with light? Violence burnishes
the body, sometimes, though we
call it damage, not burnishing, more
its opposite, a kind of darkness, as if
to hide the body, so that what's been

done to it might, too, stay hidden,
the way meaning can, for years, until
some pattern by which to trace it
at last emerges. There's a rumor of light.

This Far In

Like any spell for bringing
everyone you've ever loved back,
said the wind last night. What is it,
about nighttime and fragment
seeming made for each other? It's
morning, now. The wind is just
wind again, saying nothing, of
course. The bomb cyclone, as it's
called when there's a more powerful
than usual mash-up of warm
and cold air leading to "hurricane-
force wind events" hasn't
        happened yet, but there's an
ominous bending and failing to rise
up that the bamboo keeps doing,
that makes me think Sure,
anything could happen, but when
isn't that true? So many poems
waiting for flight, grounded
variously until better weather
or until the latest glitch (in vision,
technique, both) that caused the latest
disaster gets worked out, the way
it can seem impossible, during
the intricate steps of dressage,
that the horses ever do things like

trot into a barn or casually walk
to any field's other end—yet
they do, eventually. What's difficult
resolves. Disaster is almost

    never tragedy. The snowbells
(that appeared overnight? or am I
just now noticing them?) are only
snowbells if I call them that. I
could as easily call them Don't
tell me the worst I'd expected
is true, or Lo, the queen's bodice,
borne unobtrusively aloft, or—
or I can say it's spring again,
with its first shy flowers, meaning
color, not bearing. Not mood.
Hopkins thought flowers expressed
devotion the only way they could:
they turn toward the sun. From
humans, he suggested, God expects
more—no, is *owed* more, because
we have more to give. Leaving
out God and science,
I suppose I get that, a version
maybe of what Campion says: All

    do not all things well—as in we do
what we can. I had a house
near the sea, once, for example;
now I live where there's no sea
at all, in a house with a yard filled
with trees, among them this

barren pear tree from which I long ago
hung a set of wind chimes
designed to sound like a cross
between a ship's bells and the sort of
music tapped out by the rigging's
cable blocks as they hit their
masts unobstructed, sails down
in a storm. If I close my eyes, it really
can seem I'm home again—the sea
not far, the wind in the leaves
standing in for the waves getting
rougher than forecast, Rough
    the way once you liked it, I can
almost hear the waves choiring
back at me like an accusation
of what I don't deny, nor am I
shamed of it, bring the boats
to shore, friends, lay me down
on the shore. This far into the country,
though, a boat's pretty much
useless. Hence the pioneers with their
teetered wagons, that they
called prairie schooners out of
sheer nostalgia, already missing
the sea. *Is* that nostalgia? Or is it
more like what Xenophanes says,
how if cows could draw, the gods
in their pictures would have
horns, the gods of birds
would have feathers everywhere,

each would brandish, for
stateliness, two wings for mastering
a wind strong enough to bring
the stars down, as we used to say, before
to touch meant collision, back
when sex was what mattered

    most; seemed to. Now precision does—
specifically, that precision
with which love, felt honestly,
deploys itself as if it hadn't
planned to. So that it feels like
chance: chance as a boy with a sash
marked *Fate* across the promise
that his chest is, or soon
will be, give it time, there's time,
still. The truth is, there aren't that
many people I can say I *have* loved,
not in any way that matters
or stands memorable, really, and
of those few I'm not so certain
I'd bring any of them back. At
best, they wouldn't find me
anything close to who I was
when I loved them, which is to say
I'd disappoint them all over again,
just differently, so there'd at

    least be that. What is happening,
they used to ask me. Could you
rephrase the question, I'd sort of
mumble back, in a way it was

like dancing, when both people
know *how* to dance, what I
mean is there was grace to it,
a real grace, despite the mumbling,
which is maybe why it took so long,
for one of us to stop, if here
to stop doesn't have to mean
letting go; more like: I am grateful
for you, let neither of us wish for
or do the other harm. Let sex—
for, though I meant what I said
about it not mattering most now,
it still matters—let sex be governed
by that same restraint from
any harm unasked for. It almost
sounds like prayer sometimes,

     he said, describing light on water.
He said it like the sort of thing,
after sex, one simply says. Entering
the body, pulling gently back
out of it—is that so little for a life
to have come to? That, and
the more than a few names long
since scattered like those leaves
across which the Sibyl's prophecies
are written clearly enough,
if only the leaves would stop
moving, if I could read and know,
for once, what?—what's left for me,
in terms of time, directions

of fortune, who I am? Who am I,
the hero says to himself,
looking past his reflection
on the lake's surface down to where
the darker greens give way at last
to darkness. A light wind stirs
the surface. The reflection trembles
without breaking apart. As if
this late in the long apprenticeship,
"When I Change My Life"
had stopped being a song
anymore worth singing. I believe
and refuse to believe that,
equally. Speak to me; speak *into* me,
the wind said, when I woke
this morning, Let's see what happens.

SELECTED POEMS, 2007– 2020

FROM

SPEAK LOW

Speak Low

The wind stirred—the water beneath it stirred accordingly . . .
The wind's pattern was its own, and the water's also. The
water in that sense was the wind's reflection. The wind was,
to the water, what the water was to the light that fell there,
or appeared to fall, spilling as if the light were a liquid, or as
if the light and the water it spilled across

                          were now the same.
It is true that the light, like the water, assumed the pattern of
what acted upon it. But the water assumed also the shape
of what contained it, while the light did not. The light seemed
fugitive, a restiveness, the less-than-clear distance between
everything we know we should do, and all the rest—all
the rest that we do. Stirring, as the wind stirred it, the water
was water—was a form of clarity itself, a window we've
no sooner looked through than we've abandoned it for what
lies past that: a view, and then what comes

                          into view, or might,
if we watch patiently enough, steadily—so we believe, wishing
for what, by now, even we can't put a name to, but feel certain
we'll recognize, having done so before. It looked, didn't it,
just like harmlessness. A small wind. Some light on water.

Mirror, Window, Mirror

Yes, any sky at night, when the flickering of snow-lightning gently
punctuates it, whatever it is when it's
not bewilderment, or daring, and
not fear either, also
the mottled bark of sycamores
in autumn for where the skin
was like that. Yes.

—But more like arousal,

or more instead like the mind just
before the idea of arousal courses
bluntly through it?

That part about the body
asking for it,

to be broken into—is that the first, or last part?

Captivity

I

In the book of the body that is yours—where it's never as late
as I had thought it was, though I routinely fail, forget still
not to call it my own—

                    in the book of my body that is finally
yours only, the wind picks up, the clouds of everything that
I've been wrong about in this life pass singly overhead as if
for review, their cast
                shadows meanwhile, with the unstable
camaraderie of exiles from the start united solely in their desire,
for now, to be anywhere else, little more than that,
                              pass also . . .

Oh, sometimes it is as if desire itself had been given form, and
acreage, and I'd been left for lost there. Amazement grips me,

I grip it back, the book shuts slowly: Who shuts it? You?

II

Memory, awareness. Expectation. A light rain falls . . . That
there are three of us in the room
                        isn't clear at first, though it is
always the three of us, naked, strangers who nevertheless belong

together, but so briefly, I've no sooner assigned names to what
happens here, the names detach, reassign themselves: this one,
and now this one . . .

It makes little difference, any more than
vision does, in a room this dark. It's not by vision I tell apart
the two of them, but how the one smells like something checked
coming gradually unchecked, neither rage exactly, nor triumph

mixed with it, but not unlike that; to the other a touch that brings
everything back: the promises in their not-yet-broken state,
the brokenness after; the distilled sorrow, inside that—

∎

—How delicately, as if with care, the dark holds the nakedness that
is the three of us, turning each to each, unappeasable, in constellation . . .

In a Perfect World

Equally, the black lake that the skiff sails across,
and the skiff also. Wingbeat. A belief in evil
having not yet displaced entirely a belief in the power
to turn evil away. Laughter. Any number of small
voices in a field unfolding. Patterns like the one
where arrogance leads to shame, shame to anger,
until from anger—via the suffering called loss, called

grieving for it: at last, compassion. Hoofbeat. Bluegrass.
Persuasion slowly brushstroking its way back into
what had seemed the world. A shadow prowling
the not-so-clear-anymore perimeter of *Who says so?*
A single mother-of-pearl stud catching parts of the light—
for now, holding them. Troy is burning. Let us
make of what's left a sturdiness we can use to the end.

Distortion

Having opened to their fullest, they opened further—
Now the peonies, near to breaking, splay groundward,
some even touch the ground, and though I do understand,
yes, that they're not the not-so-lovely-after-all example
of how excess, even in its smallest forms, seems to have
its cost, I think it anyway,

                 I even think they look, more
than a little bit, like rough sex once it's gone where, of
course, it had to—do you know what I mean, his smell
on you after, like those parts of the gutted deer that
the men bring home with them, fresh from the hunt,
as if you were like that now, the parts, not the smell, I
mean as if you were his, all you'd ever wanted to be,
and how you almost believe that?

                    Do you see that too?

According to Augustine, it's a distortion of the will
that leads to passion, a slavish obedience to passion that
leads to habit, until habit in turn becomes hunger, a need.
—What is it about logic, when delivered unflinchingly,
that makes a thought like that sound true, whether true
or not? Significant of nothing but a wind that, rising
suddenly, falls as suddenly again back, the trees swing

briefly in the same direction, as if I couldn't quite
admit, yet, to a kind of grace

in synchronicity, and had
asked for proof, and the trees were one part of it, another
the light at this late-afternoon hour when it works both
against and in the body's favor, like camouflage—which
in the end is only distortion by a prettier name. I know
all about that. You can call it heartlessness, an indifference
to ruin, a willed inability to be surprised by it—you'd be
mistaken. Don't go. Let me show you what it looks like
when surrender, and an instinct not to, run side by side.

Storm

From the waist down, at least,
nothing unfamiliar. Cypress trees. The catalpa,
its seedpods hanging like shadow-icicles. And the light
around them. And the bodies that

                         enter the light, and leave it,
your own among them, but as when the body seems
most to want, impossibly, to step free of itself, oblivion
of wish,

       of wishing. —About sanctuary, how over
time it makes the birds come closer: how that's different
from trust—isn't it? *What the fuck do you think you're
looking at*, he says softly. What a thing

                 to say—
The mind protecting itself by shutting down an intimacy
that, most likely, won't be returned. Why expect it? As if
that were the mind's chief purpose, to resist a fall, though
falling's what the body

            does best. Is quick to rise for. Moving
toward you with all the ceremony of many wings at
once outspread, a holiday, descending. The dark adjusts
itself, settles its wings inside you. The shadows that
strut the dark

       open and fold like hope, a paper fan, violence
in its pitch and fall, like waves—above them, the usual
seabirds, their presumable

         indifference to chance, its

blond convergences . . . As when telling cruelty apart
from chivalry can come to seem irrelevant, or not anymore
the main point. He touches himself here,

and here. Directive.
Turns his face away. It can look like ransom. Now it looks
like privilege, now recklessness, now triumph, gravel-and-blood,
humiliation, lovely, now strict refrain, he taketh my hand
in his.

Now in Our Most Ordinary Voices

There's a kind of shadowland that one body makes, entering
another; and there's a shadowland the body contains always
within itself, without resolution—as mystery a little more
often, perhaps, should be . . . For a moment, somewhere
between the two, I can see myself as I begin to think
you must see me: a stranger to helplessness,
spouting things like *To know is to live flayed* and *Ambition
means turning the flesh repeatedly back—toward the whip,
not away*, I can still hear myself saying that, believing it—
now it all sounds wrong . . .

                    Look at the trees: willows, mostly—
They move in that way willows move—as if wanting to
pace themselves, slow, impossibly, in a building wind, as if
the wind were fate, and the trees' response one that could
maybe make a difference. Frankly, it's the inevitability part
that I most adore, still, in the inevitable. It makes of blame
an irrelevance. We'll take up once more the two positions that—
favoring depth over range—we've mastered, finally: this time it's
your turn to be the bonfire; I'll be the distance through which
the bonfire, unspecifiable, could at first be any small point
of restlessness—lit, contained—in a blackening field.

The Raft

Color of rust, russet. Color of fall. I can lay my head
on the wet sand that is nobody's chest now—not a chest,
at all—or I can lift it. Why not lift it? More fugitive than
lost, more spent than stranded, if I've been no stranger
to disillusionment,

                            nor am I enslaved to it. *The one who*
wanted me just to hold him gently, the one whose mouth
was his only tenderness, the one with whom, about whom—
who was a light, as off of water, that kept unsettling like
thought itself, like the scrim of thinking when pierced
suddenly by what nothing but instinct, pure gut, explains—

Inside me, the old desires half-negotiate, half-meander
their way back again, find those places they never stray
too far from, or not for long. I had thought the truth
would be a falcon—for how it rarely soars, as much as for
that precision with which, on wings instead built for speed
mainly, it descends, then strikes. But it is not a falcon.
The truth is a raft, a rough-at-each-of-its-edges affair of many
sturdinesses lashed together. Standard beauty; realized
expectation. The lucky ones get to choose, and they choose
when they want to. From this distance, it's hard to tell at first.
The raft's moving closer, I think. Though it's still far away.

DOUBLE SHADOW

Fascination

Guttering in its stone urn from a century, by now,
too far away, the candle made of the room
a cavernousness. The shape of the light getting cast
upward, onto the room's ceiling, became a kind
of moon, some
                    overlooked, last round of desire—
unclaimed, searching . . .

■

                There are places, still, that
no moonlight ever quite conquers: a thickness of brush,
the crossed limbs of cathedral pines,
                      defend the dark,
inside which—beneath it—the trapped fox has stopped
mutilating its own body to at last get free. Has stopped trying.
Consigns the rust-colored full length of itself to the frosted ground.

Continuous Until We Stop

But when I came to what I'd been told
was the zone of tragedy—transition—it was
not that. Was a wildering field, across it the light
steadily lessening, and the tall grasses, waving,
deepened their colors: blue-green, or
a greenish blue . . . hard to tell, exactly. Was like
when the body surrenders to risk, that moment
when an unwillingness to refuse can seem

no different from an inability to,
though they are not the same—inability,
unwillingness. To have said otherwise
doesn't make it true, or even make it count
as true. *Yes, but what does the truth
matter now*, I whispered, stepping further inside what,
by then, was night, almost. The tamer animals
would soon lie down again, and the wild go free.

The Grass Not Being Flesh, Nor Flesh the Grass

Like one of those moths, palpable
just to look at, but as if weightless as dust,
colorless
   as dust, landing on the sleeper's
mouth in the dream of darkness—and then the dark,
for real—he came to me. *Rest*, I said; and for many years,
between love and a way of loving—for they are not
the same—it is true,
     he did rest. Fluttering moth, all the more
attractive for the torn, the battered parts. As with
the others before, and since then. Him turning, or
sometimes
   I did: birch leaves when, in a gust of storm,
they'll show the side that's silver, in the same way that
certain hard mistakes do, though less
unexpectedly. Aren't they
     always fluttering? *Rest*, I say,
each night—to each of them. And in the dream, I'm resting.

The Need for Dreaming

As a scar commemorates what happened,
so is memory itself but a scar. As in: *Given*
hunger, which is endless only until it isn't, he
destroyed what he could. And then?—

So the lover enters the beloved—enters,
and withdraws; so a yellow-crested
night heron wades into view, then out:
useless? It gets harder to say. Like
signs of struggle in a field where nothing
stirs, the past can seem everywhere. I think
to be useless doesn't have to mean
not somehow mattering. Years now, and

still I can't stop collecting the strewn shells
of spent ammunition where I come across them;
carefully, I hold each up toward what's left of the light.

Almost Tenderly

It had the heft of old armor—like a breastplate
of bronze; like a shield, on hinges. It swung apart
like a door. Inside it, the sea was visible—the sea
and, on the shore, a man: stripped; beaten. Very
gently—tenderly, almost—as if to the man, to
calm him, but in fact to no one, the sea was singing:
Here, in the deepening blue of our corruption, let

love be at least one corruption we chose together.
But the man said nothing. *Why not call restlessness*
our crown, and our dominion, sang the sea . . . But
the man was a brokenness like any other: moving,
until it fails to move—the way, over time, suffering
makes no difference. His wounds were fresh; still open.
Where the light fell on them, they flashed, like the sea.

Glory On

So there's a rustling in the grass that is not what
rustles from within the fir trees—unadorned, trans-
fixed, aromatic—so what. Show me a longing
that's got no history to it, that steep glide into
what it meant once, to have glided steeply, and I'll
show you belief as a thing that's touchable: go ahead,
touch it; try to . . . Brokenness, you do surprise me—
here I could have sworn I'd lost my taste for you,
you being an accident like all the others that, one
by one, constellate, first becoming a life, and then
as if the only one, as if no other were possible. Since
when does that make a world? Whose business
but mine is it if now, when I grieve, I grieve
this way: crown in hand, little flowers of gold?

Civilization

◼

There's an art
    to everything. How
the rain means
    April and an ongoingness like
    that of song until at last

it ends. A centuries-old
    set of silver handbells that
once an altar boy swung,
    processing . . . *You're the same*
    wilderness you've always

been, slashing through briars,
    the bracken
of your invasive
    self. So he said,
    in a dream. But

the rest of it—all the rest—
    was waking: more often
than not, to the next
    extravagance. Two blackamoor
    statues, each mirroring

the other, each hoisting
    forever upward his burden of

hand-painted, carved-by-hand
   peacock feathers. *Don't*
   you know it, don't you know

I love you, he said. He was
   shaking. He said:
I love you. There's an art
   to everything. What I've
   done with this life,

what I'd meant not to do,
   or would have meant, maybe, had I
understood, though I have
   no regrets. Not the broken but
   still-flowering dogwood. Not

the honey locust, either. Not even
   the ghost walnut with its
non-branches whose
   every shadow is memory,
   memory . . . As he said to me

once, *That's all garbage*
   down the river, now. Turning,
but as the utterly lost—
   because addicted—do:
   resigned all over again. It

only looked, it—
   It must only look

like leaving. There's an art
   to everything. Even
   turning away. How

eventually even hunger
   can become a space
to live in. How they made
   out of shamelessness something
   beautiful, for as long as they could.

Immaculate Each Leaf, and Every Flower

And everywhere the smaller birds again noising, filling
steadily all the cracks between spells of rain . . .

■

As if song could still mean something useful.

■

Or a kind of pleasure that, like forgiveness, came easily and,
summer storm that forgiveness is, passed quickly through.

■

And the undersong that has been your own voice saying *No—
No I'm not afraid.*

■

What we cannot do

What we cannot undo

All the work we must do

■ ·

As for ruin—yes, but faintly.

■

The gray of doves. The gray of doves, in shadow.

Heaven and Earth

For days now, vertigo. Conqueror birds. Place where
suffering and a gift for it for a moment meet,
then go their separate ways. *I keep meaning to stop,
to wait for you.* Places where, all but untrackably, fear—
which is animal, and wild, and almost always
worth trusting—becomes cowardice: fear given
consciousness of a finite existence in the realm
of time—what exists,

                          and doesn't. Last night,
a stillness like that of moss; like permission when it's
not been given, yet not withheld exactly. Across the dark—
through it—the occasional handful of notes: someone
else out there, singing? or myself singing,
and the echoing after? I didn't know,

                                    or want to. A map
unfolding, getting folded back up again, seeming
sometimes—even as I held it—to be on fire:
It had seemed my life. What am I, that I should stand
so apart from my own happiness? The stars did
what they do, mostly: looked unbudging, transfixed,
like cattle asleep in a black pasture, all the restlessness
torn out of them, away, done with. I turn beneath them.

FROM

SILVERCHEST

So the Mind Like a Gate Swings Open

When it comes to what, eventually, it must come to,
don't forget to say to yourself *Has it come to this again*
already? Look a little lost, maybe,
                            but unsurprised.
Sometimes it feels like being a carousel horse, but
with all the paint gone strange-like, all the wood gone
driftwood, all the horses I've corralled inside me set free,
confused now, because now what? The snow fell like
hope when it's been forsaken, just before the wind shifts—
then the wind shifts, the snow flies upward . . . I love you
means what, exactly? In the end, desire may turn out
to be no different from any other song—
                            sing, and be at
last released from it. Not so long ago as I'd like to think,
I used to get drunk in parking lots with strangers: we'd park,
we'd drink, and—and didn't think what to call it, the rest
that came after, what is a thing like that worth calling: he
took me into his arms? he held me? I know longing's
a lot like despair: both can equal everything you've ever
hoped for, if that's how you want it—sure, I get that. *What's*
wrong with me, I used to ask, but usually too late, and not
meaning it anyway. He touches me, or I touch him, or don't.

After the Afterlife

Bones, for sure. Feathers almost the white
of an eagle's undershaftings in its first year.
Any wind, that stirs. Punishment in death
as it is in trembling: how it lifts, descends,
though—like having meant to be kind, yet
failing anyway—it can do no good. After
the afterlife, there's an afterlife. A stand of
cottonwood trees getting ready all over again,
because it's spring, to release their seeds that
only look like cotton; they're not cotton, at all.
What we lose, without thinking to; what we
give, for free. Distinctions that, if they even
did before, now don't matter. Any shadows
that break break randomly across these waters.

Black Swan on Water, in a Little Rain

Seen this way,
through that lens where need
and wanting swim at random

toward each other, away again, and
now and then together, he moves less like
a swan—black, or otherwise—than like any

man for whom sex is, or has at last become,
an added sense by which to pass ungently but more
entirely across a life where, in between the silences,

he leaves what little he's got to show for himself
behind him in braids of water, green-to-blue wake of
Please and *Don't hurt me* and *You can see I'm hurt, already.*

Neon

A boy walks out into a grayish distance, and he never comes back.
Anger confusable with sorrow, sorrow canceling all the anger out . . .
It's the past, and it isn't. It's forever. And it isn't. The way, in hell,
flickering's what they say what's left of the light does—a comfort,
maybe, and maybe not. Sometimes by innocence I think I've meant
the innocence of carnivores, raised in the wild, for whom the killing
is sportless, clean, unmetaphysical—then I'm not so sure. Steeplebush
flourished by some other name, lost now, long before there were
steeples. I think we ruin or we save ourselves. Comes a day when
the god, what at least you've called a god, takes you not from behind,
the usual, but pins you instead, his ass on your chest, his cock in your
face, his mouth twisting open, saying *Lick my balls*, and because you
want to live, in spite of everything, you do what he says, heaven and
earth, some rain, a few stars appearing, harder, the way he tells you to,
then not so hard, a tenderness like no tenderness you've ever shown.

Your Body Down in Gold

You can make of the world's parts something
elemental, you can say the elements mean
something still worth fucking a way forward for:
maybe the dream coming true; maybe the dream,
true to form, coming undone all over again—
you can do that, or not, while a sail unfurls,
or a door
        blows shut . . . So it turns out there's more
of a difference between love and deep affection
than you'd have chosen. So what? Remember
the days of waking to disasters various, and of
at least in part your own doing, and saying
aloud to no one *I have decided how I would
like to live my life, and it isn't*
                this way, and
how you actually believed it: you'd change,
the world would? Man with a mourning dove in
one eye, rough seas in the other, lately the light—
more than usual, it seems—finds us brokenly. I say
let's brokenly start shouldering the light right back.

Anyone Who Had a Heart

I know a man who routinely asks
that I humiliate him. It's sex, and it isn't—
whatever. For him, it's a need, the way
brutality can seem for so long a likely
answer, that
    it becomes the answer—
a kindness, even, and I have always
been kind, for which reason it goes
against my nature to do what he says, but
there's little in nature that won't, with
enough training, change . . .
      After it's done,
if the weather's good, we tour his garden:
heliotrope, evening primrose . . . *Proximity's
one thing*, he likes to say, *penetration
another*, and I have learned that's true,
though which is better depends: whose life?
what story? the relief
     of snowmelt,
or the flooded fields again? We go down
to the stables to visit the horses that,
when they were nothing, just shivering
foals still, he once asked me to give
names to. How long we've traveled,
he and I—more like
    drifted, really—and

how far. More black than all the sorrows
and joys put together that I can remember
when I try remembering, which I mostly don't,
now the foals,

          they're stallions. Call out
Fanfare, Adoration. Like broken kings,
they lower their heads, then raise them.

Dominion

Sometimes I take the leather hood off—I
refuse to wear it. As if I were king. Or a man
who's free. Ravens, red-tailed hawks, the usual
flocks of drifting-most-of-the-time strangers
settle the way even things that drift

                              have to, and
I don't care. All over again, I know things that
nobody knows, or wants to—things that, though
prettier, maybe, against the snow

                         of memory, can
still hurt, all the same. Any blame falling where
it falls—that random. That moment each day
when the light traveling across what's always been
mine to at any point take back, or give elsewhere,
becomes just the light again, turning back to dark,
when the branches

                       stir as they've stirred forever,
more tenderly over some of us than others. Sing,
or don't sing. Help me take this leather hood off—
I refuse to wear it. I'm the king. I'm free.

But Waves, They Scatter

From beneath the ice field, longing looks up at the lovers
who—variously meandering, stalling or not, fucking
or not—guess nothing of him. Torturer sometimes. Known
also to have been a savior eventually, hard passage to a life
worth the hardness. You would think longing lived in a space
warmer than an ice field, you would think so. Tragedies are
happening everywhere in the world, beside things that aren't
technically tragedies, though they include suffering, pain, death
in its more humiliating versions, to remind that some of us
will be less spared, and some will not. Up through the ice field,
longing watches the lovers who, in turn, look down, or away,
laughing. Each time, they miss the ice field for the flowers that,
despite the cold, somehow grow there: distraction's the bluer
and more abundant flower, black at the edges. Joy is the other.

Silverchest

Unafraid is what we were, I think, and then afraid,
though it mostly seemed otherwise. I opened my eyes,
I saw, I closed, I shut them.
                              The usual morning glories
twist up through banks of gone-wild-by-now holly;
crickets for song, morphos for their glamour, which
is quiet—blue, and quiet . . .

You: the dark that nothing, not even the light, displaces.
You, who have been the single leaf that
won't stop tossing,
among the others.
For you.

FROM

RECONNAISSANCE

Reconnaissance

All the more elegant forms of cruelty, I'm told, begin
with patience. I have practiced patience. As for piety
being, to superstition, as what had seemed a fortress
can be to not-a-fortress-in-the-end, at all: maybe so.

—Why not move like light, reflected, across the snow?

The Darker Powers

Even if you're right,
and there's in fact a difference
between trouble unlooked-for, and
the kind of trouble we pursued,
ruthlessly, until at last
it was ours,
                    what will the difference
have been, finally? What I've
called the world continues
to pass for one, the room spins
same as ever, the bodies
inside it do, flightless, but
no less addicted to mastering—
to the dream of mastering—the very
boughs through which
they keep falling without
motion, almost,
that slowly, it seems they'll fall
forever, my
                    pretty consorts, to whom
sometimes—out of pity,
not mercy, for
nothing tender
about it—I show the darker
powers I've hardly shown

to anyone: *Feel the weight of them,*
I say, before putting them back,
just behind my heart, where they blacken
and thrive.

Steeple

Maybe love really does mean the submission of power—
I don't know. Like pears on a branch, a shaking branch,
in sunlight, 4 o'clock sunlight, all the ways we do harm,
or refrain from it, when nothing says we have to . . . Shining,
everyone shining like that, as if reality itself depended
on a nakedness as naked as naked gets; on a faith in each
other as mistaken as mistaken tends to be, though I have
loved the mistake of it—still do; even now—as I love
the sluggishness with which, like sacrifice, like the man
who, having seen, no, having understood himself at last,
turns at first away—has to—the folded black-and-copper
wings of history begin their deep unfolding, the bird itself,
shuddering, lifts up into the half-wind that comes after—
higher—soon desire will resemble most that smaller thing,
late affection, then the memory of it; and then nothing at all.

Capella

I

I miss the sea.

I miss the storms
that stopped there.

How much is luck, again opening,
and luck shutting itself down, what we
never expected, or only sort of did,
or should have?

The windfalls of my mistakes sweetly rot beneath me.

Two hawks lift—headed north—from my highest bough.

So he's seen the blizzard that the future
looks like, and gotten lost,
a little. All the same—

he gathers the honeysuckle in his arms,
as for a lover. Cloud of bees,
of yellow.

His chest, blurring bright with it.

Who's to say brutality's what he'll be wearing,
when he goes?

III

There's a light that estrangement,
more often than not, briefly
leaves behind it.

            Then the dark—blue and damned,
erotic: here, where—done at last
with flashing like
power itself at first, then what power

comes to—the field
lays down its winded swords. —My head;
beside yours.

For Long to Hold

Not because there was nothing to say, or we
didn't want to—we just stopped speaking
entirely, but like making a gift of it: *Here;*
   for you. Saturday birds picked the sidewalk's
reminders of Friday night's losses, what got left
behind. I've been wrong about more than, despite
   memory, I had thought was possible. I keep
making my way through the so-called forests of the so-
called dead, I whistle their branches into rivers
   elsewhere, they tell the usual lies that water, lately,
can hardly wait to begin singing about: love as
rescue, rescue as to have been at last set free. If
   that's how it always seems anyway, so what,
that it did? When I whistle again—not so hard
this time, more softly—each lie blows out, then
   away: lit candles; dust. —I take everything back.

Foliage

Cage inside a cage inside a whispering so deep that
—And then just the two of us. And you calling it
vulnerability. And me calling it rumor passing
through suspicion's fingers—ashweed, flickering
halo of the boy I might really have been once, tiger
lilies beneath a storm blowing into then out of
character, then back again, as if seasonal, summer
now, now fall. But I know suspicion has no fingers.
Vulnerability's just part of the trash that rumor leaves
behind. Wait it out long enough, the trash shifts, it
always does, in that way it's like memory lately—
I'm the fist of instinct, cool, unstoppable, you're
the dogwood's crucifix-laden branches, I'm the fist
through the branches, you're the fist, I'm the branches . . .

The Strong by Their Stillness

Most mornings here, mist is the first thing to go—first
the mist, then the fog, though hardly anyone seems to know
the difference, or even care, the way for some a dead buck
is a dead buck: the road, the body, a little light, the usual
dark, light's

                unshakable escort . . . You can love a man
more than he'll ever love back or be able to, you can confuse
your understanding of that

                        with a thing like acceptance or,
worse, all you've ever deserved. I've driven hard into
the gorgeousness of spring before; it fell hard behind me:
the turning away, I mean, the finding of clothes,
the maneuvering

                awkwardly back into them . . . why not drive
forever? Respect or shame, it's pretty much your
own choice, is how it once got explained to me. I've already
said—I'm not sorry. Magnolia. Wild pear. So what if one
wish begets a next one,

                    only to be conquered by it, if the blooms
break open nevertheless like hope?

Faintly, with Falling Stars

Like having been lost unfindably, and then
not so much remembering the way, as the way
itself somehow opening: *Watch me*. And you
understanding at last—not just knowing it—
the difference, for there
                          is a difference, power
being one thing, survival another. If he
never believed you did, can you really say
you loved him, and what you say be true?

At the water's edge—as at the edge of ruin,
the kind that's meant to be looked back on once,
then it's gone, forgotten—you lift two fingers.
Your eyes shift eastward. Conquest. And,
by whatever name, the glittering
                                  slaves that
always follow conquest, like a bridal train. How
flushed the bride looks, pulling your broken face
—not untenderly—toward hers, less broken.

Spring

❖

Pointing first to the rock bluffs, then the raptors that
hovered there, and then to their eyes that—made for
hunting—flashed like shattered quartz, pulled up wild
from the sea, the fog having lifted, hours, centuries ago,
Choose one, he said,
                              whispering almost; *Choose quickly*.
As between forever, and the light now fallen. The willed
suspension of belief, say, versus the color of joy outrivaling
whoever's best intentions. That's how hard it was. Any words
left that had stood for something
                              still meaning, but in the way
that moss can mean: all winter; beneath the ice and snow.

WILD IS THE WIND

Swimming

Some nights, I rise from the latest excuse for
Why not stay awhile, usually that hour when
the coyotes roam the streets as if they've always
owned the place and had come back inspecting now
for damage. But what hasn't been damaged? History
here means a history of storms rushing the trees
for so long, their bowed shapes seem a kind of star—
worth trusting, I mean, as in how the helmsman,
steering home, knows what star to lean on. Do
people, anymore, even say helmsman? Everything
in waves, or at least wave-like, as when another's
suffering, being greater, displaces our own, or
I understand it should, which is meant to be
different, I'm sure of it, from that pleasure
Lucretius speaks of, in witnessing from land
a ship foundering at sea, though more and more
it all seems related. I love the nights here. I love
the jetty's black ghost-finger, how it calms
the harbor, how the fog hanging stranded just
above the water is fog, finally, not the left-behind
parts of those questions from which I half wish
I could school my mind, desperate cargo,
to keep a little distance. An old map from when
this place was first settled shows monsters
everywhere, once the shore gives out—it can still
feel like that: I dive in, and they rise like faithfulness
itself, watery pallbearers heading seaward, and
I the raft they steady. It seems there's no turning back.

Brothers in Arms

The sea was one thing, once; the field another. Either way,
something got crossed, or didn't. Who's to say, about
happiness? Whatever country, I mean, where *inconceivable*
was a word like any other lies far behind me now. I've
learned to spare what's failing, if it can keep what's living
alive still, maybe just

                            a while longer. Ghost bamboo that
the birds nest in, for example, not noticing the leaves, color
of surrender, color of poverty as I used to imagine it when
I myself was poor but had no idea of it. I've always thought
gratitude's the one correct response to having been made,
however painfully, to see this life more up close. *The higher*
gods having long refused me, let the gods deemed lesser
do the best they can—so a friend I somewhere along the way
lost hold of used to drunkenly announce, usually just before
passing out. I think he actually believed that stuff; he must
surely, by now, be dead. There's a rumored

                                        humbling effect
to loss that I bear no trace of. It's not loss that humbles me.
What used to look like memory—clouds for hours breaking,
gathering, then breaking up again—lately seems instead
like a dance, one of those slower, too-complicated numbers
I never had much time for. Not knowing exactly what it's
come to is so much different from understanding that it's come
to nothing. Why is it, then, each day, they feel more the same?

Musculature

The last dog I owned, or—more humanely put, so
I'm told—that I used to live with, she'd follow me
everywhere. She died eventually. I put her down's
more the truth. It *is* the truth. And now
                              this dog—that
I mostly call Sovereignty, both for how sovereignty,
like fascination, can be overrated, and for how long it's
taken me, just to half understand that. Pretty much my
whole life. Mortality seemed an ignorable wilderness
like any other; the past seemed what, occasionally, it
still does, a version of luck when luck, as if inevitably,
gets stripped away: What hope, otherwise, for suffering?
When did honesty become so hard to step into and stay
inside of, I'm not saying
                              forever, I could last a fair time
on a small while. Sovereignty sleeps hard beside me. I
pass my hands down the full length of him, like a loose
command through a summer garden. Let those plants
that can do so lean away on their stems, toward the sun.

Not the Waves as They Make Their Way Forward

Like Virgil, Marcus Aurelius died believing that his triumphs,
when pitched against his failures, had come to very little.
I don't know. Given the messiness of most lives (humble,
legendary, all the rest in between)—their interiors,
I mean—it's hard to say he was wrong. Black night. Black
train. Freight of worries. Things that stay
the same. Having reached that point that even
the luckiest sometimes never get close to, where
desire at last offers nothing more—nor less—than
what restraint can, Marcus Aurelius wrote down
some thoughts meant apparently only for himself, though
they became *Meditations*, a book without which, by now,
he'd pretty much be forgotten. It begins with gratitude.
How it ends is painful, if I'm remembering right. But it isn't pain.

Gold Leaf

To lift, without ever asking what animal exactly it once belonged to,
the socketed helmet that what's left of the skull equals
up to your face, to hold it there, mask-like, to look through it until
looking through means looking back, back through the skull,
into the self that is partly the animal you've always wanted to be,
that—depending—fear has prevented or rescued you from becoming,
to know utterly what you'll never be, to understand in doing so
what you are, and say no to it, not to who you are, to say no to despair.

What I See Is the Light Falling All Around Us

To have understood some small piece of the world
more deeply doesn't have to mean we're not as lost
as before, or so it seems this morning, random bees
stirring among the dogwood blossoms, a few here
and there stirring differently somehow, more like
resisting stillness . . . Should it come to winnowing
my addictions, I'd hold on hardest, I'm pretty sure,
to mystery, though just yesterday, a perfect stranger
was so insistent that I looked familiar, it seemed
easier in the end to agree we must know each other.
To his body, a muscularity both at odds and at one
with how fragile everything else about him, I thought,
would be, if I could see inside. What's the word
for the kind of loneliness that can feel like swimming
unassisted in a foreign language, for the very first time?

If You Go Away

When death finds me, if there be sight
at all, let me see as the torn
coyote does, turning its head
briefly, looking not with understanding but
    recognition at where the flesh falls open around
a wound that more resembles
the marsh violet's petals, that hard-to-
detect-at-first darkening that happens—soft,
steadily—toward the flower's throat. Why not
    let go of it, I used to think, meaning that
instinct by which the body shields itself
from what threatens it unexpectedly—a fist,
the next so-called unbearable
question that's bearable after all, voilà,
    surprise . . . I know death's
an abstraction, but I prefer
a shape to things, though the shapes
are changeable. In my latest version,
    death is a young man with a habit for using
one side of his mouth to blow his hair slightly
up from his brow, while with the other half he
mutters things like *Each time I leave,*
    it's like I've left forever. Behind him,
stray cabbage moths lifting up from
the catalpa's blossoms make it seem as if
one bloom had flown free

from the others, fluttering mirror from a clutch
    of still ones. There's a kind of love that
doesn't extend itself both ways
between two people equally because it doesn't have to.

For It Felt Like Power

They'd only done what all along they'd come
intending to do. So they lay untouched by regret,
after. The combined light and shadow of passing
cars stutter-shifted across the walls the way,
in summer,
              the night moths used to, softly
sandbagging the river of dream against dream's
return . . . Listen, it's not like I don't get it about
suffering being relative—I get it. Not so much
the traces of ice on the surface of four days'
worth of rainwater in a stone urn, for example,
but how, past the ice,
                         through the water beneath it,
you can see the leaves—sycamore—where they fell
unnoticed. Now they look suspended, like heroes
inside the myth heroes seem bent on making
from the myth of themselves; or like sunlight, in fog.

Monomoy

Somewhere, people must still do things like fetch
water from wells in buckets, then pour it out
for those animals that, long domesticated, would
likely perish before figuring out how to get
for themselves. That dog, for example, whose
refusal to leave my side I mistook, as a child,
for loyalty—when all along it was just blind . . . What
is it about vulnerability that can make the hand
draw back, sometimes, and can sometimes seem
the catalyst for rendering the hand into sheer force,
destructive? *Don't you see how you've burnt almost
all of it, all the tenderness, away*, someone screams
to someone else, in public—and looking elsewhere,
we walk quickly past, as if even to have heard
that much might have put us at risk of whatever fate
questions like that

                spring from. Estrangement—
like sacrifice—begins as a word at first, soon it's
the stuff of drama, cue the follow-up tears that
attend drama, then it's pretty much the difference
between waking up to a storm and waking up
inside one. Who can say how she got there—
in the ocean, I mean—but I once watched a horse
make her way back to land mid-hurricane: having
ridden, surfer-like, the very waves that at any moment
could have overwhelmed her in their crash to shore, she
shook herself, looked back once on the water's restlessness—
history's always restless—and the horse stepped free.

Wild Is the Wind

About what's past, *Hold on when you can,* I used to say,
And when you can't, let go, as if memory were one of those
mechanical bulls, easily dismountable, should the ride
turn rough. I lived, in those days, at the forest's edge—
metaphorically, so it can sometimes seem now, though
the forest was real, as my life beside it was. I spent
much of my time listening to the sounds of random, un-
knowable things dropping or being dropped from, variously,
a middling height or a great one until, by winter, it was
just the snow falling, each time like a new, unnecessary
taxonomy or syntax for how to parse what's plain, snow
from which the occasional lost hunter would emerge
every few or so seasons, and—just once—a runaway child
whom I gave some money to and told no one about,

having promised . . . *You must keep what you've promised
very close to your heart, that way you'll never forget*
is what I've always been told. I've been told quite
a lot of things. They hover—some more unbidden than
others—in that part of the mind where mistakes and torn
wishes echo as in a room that's been newly cathedraled,
so that the echo surprises, though lately it's less the echo
itself that can still most surprise me about memory—
it's more the time it takes, going away: a mouth opening
to say *I love sex with you too it doesn't mean I wanna stop
my life for it,* for example; or just a voice, mouthless,
asking *Since when does the indifference of the body's
stance when we're alone, unwatched, in late light, amount*

to cruelty? For the metaphysical poets, the problem
with weeping for what's been lost is that tears
wash out memory and, by extension, what we'd hoped
to remember. If I refuse, increasingly, to explain, isn't
explanation, at the end of the day, what the sturdier
truths most resist? It's been my experience that
tears are useless against all the rest of it that, if I
could, I'd forget. That I keep wanting to stay should
count at least for something. I'm not done with you yet.

The Sea, the Forest

Like an argument against keeping the more
unshakable varieties of woundedness inside, where
such things maybe best belong, he opened his eyes
in the dark. *Did you hear that*, he asked . . . I became,
all over again, briefly silver, as in what the leaves
mean, beneath, I could hear what sounded like waves
at first, then like mistakes when, having gathered
momentum, they crash wave-like against the shore of
everything that a life has stood for. —*What*, I said.

FROM

PALE COLORS

IN A TALL FIELD

On Being Asked to Be More Specific
When It Comes to Longing

When the forest ended, so did the starflowers and wild
ginger that for so long had kept us
company, the clearing opened before us, a vast
meadow of silverrod, each stem briefly an
angled argument against despair, then only weeds by
a better name again, as incidental as
the backdrop the ocean made just
beyond the meadow . . . Like taking
a horsewhip to a swarm of bees, that they might
more easily disperse, we'd at last reached the point

in twilight where twilight seems most
a bowl designed to turn routinely but
as if by accident half roughly
over: bells somewhere, the kind
of bells that, before being housed finally
in their towers, used to
have to be baptized, each was given—
to swing by or fall hushed inside of,
accordingly—its own name; bells, and then—
from the smudged edge of all that
seemed to be left of what we'd called

belief, once, bodies, not of hunting-birds, what we'd
thought at first, but human bodies in flight,

in flight and lit from within as if
by ruin, or triumph, maybe, at having
made out of ruin a light, something
useful by which, having skimmed the water, to search
the meadow now, for ourselves inside it where, yes, though we
shook in our nakedness, we lay
naked as we'd been taught to do: when afraid,
what is faith, but to make a gift of yourself—give; and you shall receive.

Pale Colors in a Tall Field

Remind me to show you where the horses finally got freed
for good—not for the freedom of it, or anything like
beauty, though their running was for sure a loveliness, I'm
thinking more how there's a kind of violence to re-entering
unexpectedly a space we never meant to leave but got
torn away from so long ago it's more than half forgotten,
not that some things aren't maybe best forgotten, at a
certain point at least, I've reached that point in my own life
where there's so much I'd rather not remember, that
to be asked to do so can seem a cruelty, almost; bad enough,
some days, that there's memory at all, though that's not
exactly it, it's more what gets remembered, how we
don't get to choose. For example, if love used to mean
rescue, now it's more gladiatorial, though in the end
more clean: Who said that? Not the one whose face I've
described somewhere as the sun at that moment when,
as if half unwilling, still, to pull itself free from the night's
shadow-grove of losses, it first begins to appear. No.
Not that one. And not the one whose specialty was
making a bad habit sound more excusable by calling it
ritual—since when do names excuse? Wish around for it
hard enough, you can always find some deeper form
of sadness where earlier—so at least you thought—mere
sorrow lay . . . I'd been arguing the difference between
the soul being cast out and the soul departing, so I
still believed in the soul, apparently. It was that long ago.

For Nothing Tender About It

If as shame is to memory, so too desire,
then is this desire, this cloak of shadows,
that I wrap close around me, that I
refuse to take off?

But the lake looks endless.
And my boat's increasingly but a slowish swimmer,
across the waves—I've known
hurt, I mean; and I have been afraid. Sometimes

the difference between forgetting
to bring along artillery and showing up
on purpose to the war unarmed

is just that: a difference. Sometimes a lost tune,
unreckoned on, unearned, resurfaces anyway. Just because.

Am I not the animal by belief alone I myself make possible?

Dirt Being Dirt

The orchard was on fire, but that didn't stop him from slowly walking
straight into it, shirtless, you can see where the flames have
foliaged—here, especially—his chest. Splashed by the moon,
it almost looks like the latest proof that, while decoration is hardly
ever necessary, it's rarely meaningless: the tuxedo's corsage,
fog when lit scatteredly, swift, from behind—swing of a torch, the lone
match, struck, then wind-shut . . . How far is instinct from a thing
like belief? Not far, apparently. At what point is believing so close
to knowing, that any difference between the two isn't worth the fuss,
finally? A tamer of wolves tames no foxes, he used to say, as if avoiding
the question. But never meaning to. You broke it. Now wear it broken.

A Little Closer Though, If You Can,
For What Got Lost Here

Other than that, all was still—a quiet
so quiet that, as if silence were a kind of spell, and
words the way to break it, they began speaking.
   They spoke of many things:
sunset as a raft leaving the water in braids behind it;
detachment, the soul, obedience;
swans rowing at nightfall across a sky filled with snow;
what did they wish they could see, that they used to see;
to mean no harm, or to not especially, just now, be looking for it;
what would they wish not to see, could they stop seeing;
courage mattering so much less than not spooking easily—
maybe all nerve is; the search-and-rescue map wildflowers
make of a field in summer; deserving it, versus asking for it,
versus having asked, and been softly turned from.
   They said it would hurt, and it does.

Yet No Less Grateful

Woke feeling like a Minotaur: hot, torn,
not so much undecided as undecided *upon*, and badly:
what can I possibly do now about what I am, if I'm what I am?

Like mistaking death for what's finally just proof of death—
the latest stubbornly unvanished body beside the road that the wide,
now sightless eye unstares across—
to rewrite what's been given is not refusal is no one walking away.

Between trust and what trust equals, between that and everything
I say it does, why not do whatever?

They say the difficulty with nothing-but-light,
as with utter darkness, is not so much that we cannot see,
but that we're stripped of context: we're as near
as far; all the waves stand frozen. I can't stop thinking of the future
as the past, imitating a god.

Is It True All Legends Once Were Rumors

And it was as we'd been told it would be: some stumbling wingless;
others flew beheaded. But at first when we looked at them, we could
see no difference, the way it can take a while to realize about how
regretfulness is not regret. As for being frightened: though for many
animals the governing instinct, when most afraid, is to attack, what about
the tendency of songbirds, in a storm, toward silence—is that fear, too?
For mostly, yes, we were silent—tired, as well, though as much out of
boredom as for the need to stretch a bit, why not the rest on foot, we
at last decided—and dismounting, each walked with his horse close
beside him. We mapped our way north by the stars, old school, until there
were no stars, just the weather of childhood, where it's snowing forever.

Overheard, Under a Dark Enchantment

Compassion first, we were told—and if that won't work,
compassion's shadow, pity, to smooth what's rough.
                                           We find
just holding the victim's hand, lately, has been exactly enough.

If It Must Be Winter

Not crowns,
not conquest defined in terms of how many fear you, or
fear to say otherwise, not by these
will you know your own royalty, but in smaller ways, how
to the least gesture there's more power than seems reasonable,
though it will feel deserved . . . So I was told, and they have not
proved wrong. I've but to open my hand,
bees come to it, the slick fur of bees
assembling as toward an honor in no way expected

though each time the honor remains mine, as if
almost it should, as if certain privileges had to do with destiny—
Do I believe that? Do I? My hand a sea
across which the wings of the bees flash
like signal flags whose patterns, instead of translating,
I make up my own translations for. I shall do as I please.
As a lovely argument can make a difficult truth
more clear, if not more sweet, though is there not
a sweetness to clarity that can almost make the truth

seem worth it? To say I'm not quite sure makes me no less
king, here. Sometimes, I open my hand and there's no sea at all,
just a windy plain, what appear to be dust storms crossing it
turn out, on reaching me, to be the disappointments—
all of them—that I never intended, each one

on horseback, my cavalry, each face
raised toward mine, as if awaiting command—
hungering for it. Forgetful, or stupid. I can see
no difference.   Look away from me. I haven't said you can look at me.

Defiance

Some say the point of war
is to make the need for tenderness

more clear. Some say that's an effect of war, the way
beauty can be: Homer's *Iliad*, for example; or—
many centuries later—how the horse's head,

to protect it in combat, would be fitted
with a shaffron, a strip of steel,
sometimes mixed with copper, all of it

hammer-worked, parts detailed
in gold. I love you, as I've

always loved you, one man says,
meaning it, to another. That doesn't make

love true. This only needs to be troubling
if we want it to be. Our minds are
as the days are, dark

or bright, says Homer, the words like coral bells
in a pot made to look like the head of an ancient god—
a sea-god, moss for seaweed across the old

god's face. To believe in ritual in the name
of hope, there lies disaster.

                            And turned to him.

And took his hand—the scarred one; I could
feel the scars . . . Little crowns. Mass

coronation. For by then all the lilies on the pond had opened.

STAR MAP WITH
ACTION FIGURES

And If I Fall

There's this cathedral in my head I keep
making from cricket song and
dying but rogue-in-spirit, still,
bamboo. Not making. I keep
imagining it, as if that were the same
thing as making, and as if making might
bring it back, somehow, the real
cathedral. In anger, as in desire, it was
everything, that cathedral. As if my body
itself cathedral. I conduct my body
with a cathedral's steadiness, I
try to. I cathedral. In desire. In anger.
Light enters a cathedral the way persuasion fills a body.
Light enters a cathedral, the way persuasion fills a body.

Dangerous Only When Disturbed

Of birdsongs, I know only three
for certain: cardinal, blue jay, raven,
though perhaps the last two
don't count—not as song. More call
than song. More cry, by which I mean
exclamatory, not the kind
with tears. Not that tears
can't be song sometimes, depending on
who's weeping, for what reason, and
with what degree of restraint, finally, at least
half of what any music worth being
called music's made of; as for the rest—
release? Does that still
sound right? Did you know the blue
of the blue morpho butterfly's
iridescent wings isn't biological
but an engineering of light, that they're
not blue at all? In the song
of you, in the song I make of you,
in which your horselessness means
a fear of horses, nothing
more than that, you're a man asleep
beneath the willow's umbrella, you've
grown your hair out, the hair rises
the way dream does to the cool
descent of the willow's branches, from

the thicket that hair and branches and
dream make, I haven't
forgotten you, it's just I've been
distracted, between the sound
of birds singing somewhere and this
inability to keep any song left
inside me from ruining
everything, or so I tell myself, and
like that, if not true as in
provable, as in *here's proof*, it's true enough
to believe in. You're awake, I think.
Your mouth is moving.

Wake Up

The road down from everything even you had hardly dared
to hope for has its lonely stretches, yes, but it's hard to feel alone
entirely: there's a river that runs beside it the whole way down,
and there's an over-song that keeps the river company: I'm leaves,
you're the wind . . .

I used to think the song had to do with the leaves'
confusion, the wind letting up, their mistaking this for something
like courtesy on the wind's part, or even forgiveness. But leaves don't
get confused. Silly, to think it. And what can leaves know of courtesy,
let alone forgiveness? What's forgiveness?

Wake up, for the falconer
has lost his falcon. He has heard that falcons are like memory, they
come back. But not all memories do, not all memories should. If
anyone knows this, it's the falconer. How long ago that was . . . Yet

all the varieties of good fortune he's come upon, as a hand comes
idly upon an orchard's windfalls, how different he's become since—
none of it matters, when the falconer steps back into memory as into
a vast cathedral, which is to say, when he remembers.

How cool it is,
inside the cathedral. And at first, how dark. Soon, though, he can see
a chapel set aside for prayers specifically to the virgin whose story he's
always resisted. He sees a corner where people have lit candles, sometimes

for another's suffering, sometimes for their own. He sees the altar with
the falcon sitting on top of it.

The weight of grief over what's lost,
versus the shadow of what's lost—forever struggling to return, and failing:
who can say which is better? The falconer's eye meets the falcon's eye:

I have a story, the falcon says, seems to, the wings lifting, the feathers
rippling with a story's parts—I have a story; I can't wait to tell you.

On Triumph

If done steadily, and with the kind of patience that belies all fear,
it is indeed possible to walk the plank backwards from the doom
of vanishing

       to that softer, wildflowered field across which mere
diminishment winds like a path maybe worth sticking to, finally, for look
where the alternatives have led—not that, even now, you regret them,
or would, if you believed in regret,

               if you could understand regret
in all of its steepness, the slim shadow it has a way of casting—like
a finger at the lips, for silence—across that chaos whose names,
so it seems, change endlessly: unreason, consciousness, the sea with its
shifting patterns, now fluorescence and glitter, now glitter and shine,
mirrors

      wasted on the usual mob that, forever strange to it, spits
on triumph as if triumph were tangible, meant both to protect the chest
and give a certain grace to it, like chain mail, but not made of metal
this time—instead, glass bells:

           so small;
    each gently hitting the next, beside it;
      plovers piping from the low seagrass that barely hides them;

Unbridled

To look at them, you might not think the two men, having spoken briefly
      and now moving away from each other, as different goals
   require, have much history, if any,
between them. That for a time that seems longer ago now than in fact
      it's been, they used to enter each other's bodies so often, so routinely,
   yet without routine ever seeming the right way of putting it,
that even they lost count—for back then,
      who counted? It's not as if they've forgotten, or at least
   the one hasn't, looking long enough back at the other
to admire how outwardly unchanged he seems: still muscled, even if
      each muscle most brings to mind (why, though)
   an oracle done hiding at last, all the mystery made
quantifiable, that it might more easily that way—like love, like the impulse
      toward love—be disassembled. The other man doesn't look back
   at all, or think to, more immediately distracted
by the dog he had half forgotten at the end of a leash he'd forgotten
      entirely, though here it is, in his hand,
   and the dog at the end of it. What kind of dog? The kind whose
digging beneath the low-lying branches of a bush thick with flowers
      shakes the flowers loose, they make of the dog's
   furious back a fury of petals that the dog takes no notice of,
though the man has noticed.
      How the petals lie patternless where they've fallen.
      How there's a breeze, bit of storm in it. How as if in response
the dog lifts its dirt-blackened face from the hole it's digging,
      then continues digging. Then the man is crying. No it *looks* like crying.
      Now what good at this point do you really think that's likely to do
either of us, he says, to the dog.

We Turn Here

If we don't have to bring honesty into this,
    why bring it, or that's at least what I
        think the question was, though what I more
remember is how it kept breaking—
     the question did—the way waves do,
        touching shore (one, that I shall be punished,
two, that this is not yet the punishment), each wave eventually
    indistinguishable from the wave before.

To Lie Down. To Wear Nothing at All.

And then just like that, with hardly anyone
noticing, it became daily harder to remember when
this sense of being at sea had begun—at sea, as in
on a wave of doubt mixed with fear and yet no small
amount, incongruously, of fevered anticipation, not joy
itself but the belief, still—the half-belief—some joy
might come. Maybe
                    the beginning doesn't matter anyway—
whatever wasn't the case once, it's the case now, long
days of jazz and drinks named after jazz, Give me a John
Coltrane, someone saying; Another, I'll take one more
round of these Take Fives . . . Not that there aren't
those who suspect the headiness of this new weather
will soon enough dissipate, the holler-and-buzz
surrounding it will follow suit. We're alike in that way,
you and I—comrades, if you will, in our shared
suspicion, whether you know it yet or not, says
the captain to the young man across the room,
who of course can't hear him because the captain has
only said this to himself, not aloud yet. He looks at
the young man,
                    who hasn't yet seen the captain. It's as if
he's trying not to look. Look at me, thinks the captain. And
the young man's head starts to turn toward him. Any
moment he'll see the captain for the first time. The way
all histories begin, apparently. What destroys finding
what will be destroyed, though which is which has yet to be
determined. Almost lavender, the captain's eyes are, in this light.

Reasonable Doubt

What it looked like?

Like fucking the forest for once birdless, beastless.

Like measuring the distance between all that's lost
and everything else that, even now, waved at
hard enough sometimes,
will sometimes wave back.

But it felt like swallowing the sea—
being forced to, ships and all.

Then a silence as vast as it was particular.

Then like holding a mirror up to Apollo
and expecting his face there, when Apollo's always been
faceless, obviously, being a god.

And the hand still holding the mirror up anyway.

And the face not showing.

Fine

I have a story. In this story, there's a set of doors,
shut, medieval—
at least they look medieval—across the blue
tops of which someone has spray-painted—
but carefully, in gold, like an updated,
somehow sluttier, therefore
sturdier version of gold leaf—two sentences:
    Tell me what enters.
    Speak of what's forever getting left behind.
Sentences that, ever since their
overnight-three-weeks-ago appearance,
no one calls sentences, everyone here
calls them prayers. How does a sentence,

just like that, become prayer? What's prayer anyway? From
a window not far but, from here, not visible, I think now
it's better, maybe, that we not speak again
ever, someone has just said to no one answering. I can't
hear an answer. It's the kind of
town, still, where no one locks the doors,

you can step inside.
Step inside.
Imagine the dreamer's difficulty—
try to: the sheer weight, of course, of dream;
the not-yet-broken-to-ride horse;

the hanged man's naked body, athletic
even now, especially now, stopped
in stillness, "Wilderness has been
no mystery" tattooed
across the dead man's chest. Feel regret—
fine—but do you have to keep speaking of it as if regret
were a game of horseshoes, or a power saw, or the sea?

And Swept All Visible Signs Away

Easy enough, to say it's dark now.
But what is the willow doing in the darkness?
I say it wants less for company than for compassion,

which can come from afar and faceless. What's a face, to a willow?
If a willow had a face, it would be a song, I think.
I am stirred, I'm stirrable, I'm a wind-stirred thing,

the song would go . . . But there
is no song. As there is no face. There's just the willow
as willow. Nothing but itself. Its shadow meaningless

except to those who want for shade,
and find it there. Who keep finding they hardly
care anymore—almost, some days, as if they'd never cared—

about connection. Green as water, the willow's motion. Green as oblivion,
the willow's indifference—flecked with a little gold, some blue.

Honest in Which Not Gently

Does it matter how festive it was, the setting out for far country,
the horses, their chestnut flanks, their eyes the color of black basil,
which is purple, really? Now just skulls where a face used to be,
shameless, as in bereft of shame finally, each catching the snow
gently but differently, the snow, and the wind scattering it, as if

unapparent meant *nonexistent*. They say language has its own sorrow,
but no word for it: does this crying out maybe come close, though,
can we say it does, to have stared into the dark and said aloud, even
if quietly, Who's there? Anyone around? Panicking too late, as is
the way with panic, the killer stumbles through woods and a snowfall

that feels like ritual and a release from ritual, so that it also feels—
at first, anyway—like being lost, but free. Beneath the pines, the two
horses stood exactly where he'd left them untethered hours ago. Snow
dusted their fine bodies. Nightmare. Nightmare Lifting. Their names
swim up to him. I remember, now. Yes. Now it's all coming back.

Self

You plan on riding with me,
you'll have to hold on tight, I told him, or
maybe he told me, whoever I must have been or thought I was in those

days that—who remembers, now, except for there being just the two
dreams left by then,
and how hard to decide: the dream of bondage,

or the other one, not of the slow release from bondage but from
any thought or desire to go, even briefly, free, for was not freedom
a kind of bondage, too? Sometimes,

they thought that. The way that, even though they understood the self
as a thing impossible to see past,
they could still think it was worth trying to, as if the self were a vast

thicket through which, sure, the light made its way occasionally but was
mostly thwarted,
or as if the self were the horizon sea and sky make

at sunset, just before sunset, and not in fact a needle pushed through
the stretched canvas of belief then pulled back
up again, up through belief, into recognition: there are choices,

you can choose. If the bruised face in the mirror isn't what you meant to see,
or you just don't right now feel like looking at it, look away.
So you look away.

Soundtrack for a Frame of Winter

There's a forest that stands at the exact center of sorrow.
Regrets find no shelter there.
The trees, when they sway,
sway like the manes of horses when a storm's not far.
There's no reason to stay there,
nothing worth going to see,
but if you want to you can pass through the forest
in the better part of a long day.
Who would want to, though?

To have entered the forest changes nothing about sorrow.
It's a forest. Not oblivion. Not erasure.
Some have entered it in the name of distraction,
if only briefly, from the sorrow within which
the forest thrives to no apparent purpose—fools, dreamers,
the desperate from whom it's best, if at all possible,
to look calmly away, the trees of the forest at the center of sorrow—
the exact center—all but say,
or that's what it sounds like on windier nights,

tonight, for example. At the forest's exact center,
almost impossible to find, but I have been there myself,
there's a makeshift grave, more than likely overgrown by now
with weeds, moss, the usual.
With defeat, desire, the usual.

Wingless ambition, frangible hope, misunderstanding, i.e., mistake,
another form of weakness, i.e., the usual.
That the forest itself contains no apology
doesn't mean you're not hurt. Or I'm not sorry. Or I didn't hurt you.

Star Map with Action Figures

More dark than gray, but not yet quite dark
entirely, the stories keep ending as if there were
a limit to what any story could hold on to, and this
the limit, the latest version of it, looking a lot like the sea
meeting shore.

■

To constellate, the way desire
does, sometimes, with fear, or anger—both, occasionally—
and there's been gentleness, too, *I'm here, I've*
always been here . . .

■

Maybe between mystery
and what little we can say for sure
happened, lies a secret even
memory itself keeps somewhere
hidden because for now
it has to.

■

Less like wishing too late, I mean,
for a thing to be otherwise than like fire closing in

so absolutely, it can almost seem intimacy
had yet to be invented, and here's the fire,
inventing it: *Constellate,*
with me—

Look at the field,
studded with the blue-black eyes of broken heroes.
One of the eyes is moving. It can still see. What does it see?

My Monster

This hill, even if a small one, this hill with us and the dog the same dog
forever moving shadowlike down it, to where the hill disappears . . . For
some of a winter long ago, back when empathy still seemed a form
of love—more static, maybe, less steep, but just as complicated—
I stayed in a small house, cabin-like, but no cabin, at the end of a pier
that jutted out into a harbor the way piers do. It was January. Why so

this quiet, he used to ask, in his language. I barely knew his language.
I'd turn him over, and there was sex or not, then, and there was
sleeping after. At night as I lay in bed, the whole place would rock,
mostly gently, which was the tide finding higher shore again, or
sometimes the wind making rough with water, as was the case one
particular night when it was snowing. Snowing over the sea,

and windy. I know resemblance is not equation. I know
equivalence doesn't mean translation. I say there was a wind,
and that's often how I remember it, but tonight it almost seems
the night must have been windless, I remember the steady verticality
with which the snow fell, falling into the sea. I'd turn him over; I barely
knew him; why so this quiet. The crown looks good on you, the veil
does too—when you lift the veil, the future's everything you wished for.

All the Love You've Got

■

And now, having dismissed everyone as he
wishes he could dismiss his own dreams that make each
night restless—that same unswayable knowledge, and
the belief in it, that he is
                                king here, which means
being a stranger, at least outwardly, to even the least
trace of doubt—after all of this, the king has stepped
from the royal tent, is walking toward the sound
of water, where the river must be. There's the river,
rivering south,
                                as rivers tend to. Beside the river,
two men are fucking. Young men. Almost too young
to even know about fucking, thinks the king, who can't
help noticing how the men bring a somehow grace
to the business between them—a grace that some might
confuse with love. But the king
                                        rarely makes mistakes,
which is to say, he knows mercy when he sees it. What
does mercy have to do with fucking? What does love
have to do with grace? What are dreams but the only
rivers memory knows how to make? There's a kind of
music
        to how the men routinely but unpredictably trade
places entering and withdrawing from each other. It's as if
they're singing a song that might go "I'm the king, no you're

the king and I'm the river, no you're the river." On and on,
like that. Leave them; they do

no harm. The king making
his slow, insomnia-ed way back. The night dark but not dark
entirely: moonless, yes, but through the pines enough stars
still visible. Whoever goes there,

let me pass. Beneath
the brocaded cloak, each bead stitched to it by hand,
beneath the cloak of some more breathable, lighter fabric
beneath that, the king's cock rests like tenderness itself
against the king's left thigh. How soft the stars look.

NOTES

THEN THE WAR

"The Enchanted Bluff" is also a short story by Willa Cather, in *Five Stories* (New York: Vintage Books, 1956).

Morning in the Bowl of Night is the title of an Alma Thomas painting, with which the poem is in conversation.

"He Didn't Raise Hand or Voice": The title is a line from Pamela Alexander's poem "The Vanishing Point," in *Navigable Waterways* (New Haven, CT: Yale University Press, 1985).

"Somewhere, right now, a hawk": Carl Jung speaks of despair as a necessary state to be passed through for the self's growth in *Psychology and Alchemy*, trans. R. F. C. Hull (Princeton, NJ: Princeton University Press, 1980).

"Among the Trees": "There's a kind of shadowland . . .": The quoted text is from my poem "Now in Our Most Ordinary Voices," in *Speak Low* (New York: Farrar, Straus and Giroux, 2009).

"Was like when the body surrenders . . .": The entire passage is from my poem "Continuous Until We Stop," in *Double Shadow* (New York: Farrar, Straus and Giroux, 2011).

"I lived, in those days . . .": The quoted text is from my poem "Wild Is the Wind," in *Wild Is the Wind* (New York: Farrar, Straus and Giroux, 2018).

"There's a forest that stands . . .": The quoted text is from my poem "Soundtrack for a Frame of Winter," in *Star Map with Action Figures* (Little Rock, AR: Sibling Rivalry Press, 2019).

"I become briefly silver . . .": A slight variation of a sentence from my poem "The Sea, the Forest," in *Wild Is the Wind* (New York: Farrar, Straus and Giroux, 2018).

"Sudden scattering, all around me . . .": A slight variation of the title of my poem "Sudden Scattering of Leaves, All Gold," in *The Rest of Love* (New York: Farrar, Straus and Giroux, 2004).

"Everything All of It": I owe my knowledge of this fact about oak trees to Jeremy Cooper's novel *Ash Before Oak* (London: Fitzcarraldo Editions, 2019).

"Of the Shining Underlife": The title borrows a phrase from Toi Derricotte's "The Minks," in *Captivity* (Pittsburgh, PA: University of Pittsburgh Press, 1989).

"Night Comes and Passes Over Me": The title is a line from Adélia Prado's poem "Mobiles," in *The Alphabet in the Park: Selected Poems*, trans. Ellen Watson (Middletown, CT: Wesleyan University Press, 1990).

"This Far In": "When I Change My Life" appears on the Pretenders' album *Get Close* (1986).

SPEAK LOW

"Speak Low": The title is that of the Billie Holiday standard, written by Kurt Weill.

"Captivity": "Amazement grips me" is from Augustine's *Confessions* [X. viii (15)], trans. Henry Chadwick (New York: Oxford University Press, 1991). In the same text, he divides human experience of time into memory, awareness, and expectation [XI. xx (26)].

"Distortion": See Augustine's *Confessions* [VIII. v (10)] for the relationship between the will, passion, habit, and hunger.

DOUBLE SHADOW

"Continuous Until We Stop": Karl Jaspers defines transition as the zone of tragedy in "Basic Characteristics of the Tragic in Tragedy," as it appears in *Tragedy: Vision and Form*, ed. Robert W. Corrigan (New York: Harper & Row, 1981).

SILVERCHEST

"Anyone Who Had a Heart" is also the title of a song by Burt Bacharach and Hal David.

RECONNAISSANCE

"Steeple": The opening sentence responds to an assertion by Gillian Rose in *Love's Work* (New York: New York Review Books, 2011).

"For Long to Hold": The title is from Hart Crane's "The Broken Tower," in *Complete Poems of Hart Crane*, ed. Marc Simon (New York: Liveright, 1993).

"The Strong by Their Stillness": The title comes from a sentence in Juan Pablo Villalobos's *Down the Rabbit Hole*, trans. Rosalind Harvey (New York: Farrar, Straus and Giroux, 2012).

WILD IS THE WIND

The italicized line in "Monomoy" is a variation on a sentence in Iris Murdoch's *The Sea, the Sea* (New York: Penguin Books, 1980).

"Wild Is the Wind": Thank you to Annelise Duerden, whose dissertation, "Mortal Verse: Memory in Early Modern Poetry of Love, Grief, and Devotion," directed me to the relationship between tears and memory in the work of Donne and his contemporaries.

PALE COLORS IN A TALL FIELD

"If It Must Be Winter": The title is from a line that ends Linda Gregg's poem "Part of Me Wanting Everything to Live," in *The Sacraments of Desire* (St. Paul, MN: Graywolf Press, 1991).

"Defiance": "Our minds are as the days are, dark or bright" is from book 18 of Homer's *The Odyssey*, trans. Robert Fitzgerald (New York: Farrar, Straus and Giroux, 1998).

STAR MAP WITH ACTION FIGURES

"And If I Fall": The title is also the title of a song by The Charlatans.
"My Monster": The title is also the title of a short story by Bo Huston.

About the Order of Poems

The poems in the "Selected Poems, 2007-2020" section of this book appear based on the order in which I wrote them. The chapbook *Star Map with Action Figures* was published a year before *Pale Colors in a Tall Field*, but I wrote the chapbook poems after having turned in the manuscript for *Pale Colors in a Tall Field*, and I immediately saw them as a separate project from that of *Pale Colors in a Tall Field*. Hence, the chapbook poems—which appear in their entirety—close this collection, being the newest of the selected poems.

ACKNOWLEDGMENTS

I am grateful for the belief and support of the journals—their editors, specifically—where these poems (some in different form) were given a home:

Academy of American Poets/Poem-a-Day: "Something to Believe In"

American Poetry Review: "Not Wild, Merely Free," "The Blue Door," "The Enchanted Bluff"

bath magg: "Rough Surf in Moonlight"

Copper Nickel: "To Autumn," "While Night Still Keeps Us"

Emergence Magazine: "Among the Trees"

Jewish Currents: "Invasive Species"

Kenyon Review: "Of California"

The Night Heron Barks: "Soft Western Light"

Oxford American: "Blue-Winged Warbler"

Peripheries (Harvard Divinity School): "Anywhere Like Peace," "Night Comes and Passes Over Me"

Plume: "In a Field, at Sunset"

Poetry: "A Little Closer Though, If You Can, For What Got Lost Here," "Archery," "Entire Known World So Far," "Of the Shining Underlife," "Then the War," "This Far In"

Quarterly West: "He Didn't Raise Hand or Voice"

The Rumpus: "On Coming Close," "That the Gods Must Rest"

The Sewanee Review: "Blurry Finally in Too Soon Each of Us," "Electric"

32 Poems: "In a Low Voice, Slowly," "Initial Descent"

Under a Warm Green Linden: "Like the Sweet Wet Earth Itself"

Washington Square Review: "Everything All of It"

Well Poetry Review: "Somewhere, right now, a hawk"

The Yale Review: "As the Rain Comes Down Harder," "Only Portions of the Map Still Legibly Survive"

ZYZZYVA: "Fixed Shadow, Moving Water," "Little Shields, in Starlight"

"*Morning in the Bowl of Night*" originally appeared in *The Map of Every Lilac Leaf: Poets Respond to the Smith College Museum of Art*, ed. Matt Donovan (Northampton, MA: Smith College Museum of Art, 2020).

"Sing a Darkness" originally appeared in *Together in a Sudden Strangeness: America's Poets Respond to the Pandemic*, ed. Alice Quinn (New York: Knopf, 2020).

"The Difficulty" originally appeared in the anthology *Plume Poetry 8*.

"On Coming Close" also appeared in *The Orison Anthology*, vol. 5, eds. Luke Hankins, Nathan Poole, and Karen Tucker (Asheville, NC: Orison Books, 2020).

"Something to Believe In" also appeared in *The Best American Poetry 2020*, eds. Paisley Rekdal and David Lehman (New York: Scribner, 2020).

"To Autumn" also appeared in *The Pushcart Prize XLVI: Best of the Small Presses*, ed. Bill Henderson (Wainscott, NY: Pushcart Press, 2021).

"In a Low Voice, Slowly" also appeared on *Verse Daily*, August 11, 2020.

"While Night Still Keeps Us" also appeared on *Verse Daily*, November 6, 2020.

Star Map with Action Figures was originally published as a chapbook (Little Rock, AR: Sibling Rivalry Press, 2019).

INDEX OF TITLES AND FIRST LINES